BONDING

WITH THE REFERENCE

TABLES

**A Clear & Simple
Chemistry Regents Guide**

Y. Finkel

What is This Book & How Do I Use It?

> This is a test of your knowledge of chemistry. Use that knowledge to answer all questions in this examination. Some questions may require the use of the *2011 Edition Reference Tables for Physical Setting/Chemistry*. You are to answer *all* questions in all parts of this examination according to the directions provided in this examination booklet.

Did you know that an average of about 34 questions in every Chemistry Regents (or about 40% of the regents) are partially or entirely based on the Chemistry Reference Tables?

If you know how to read *every* table on the Chemistry Reference Tables, that's terrific.

But what if you don't?

Gaining a clear understanding of the reference tables is crucial for the Chemistry Regents.

The good news is that one of the best-kept secrets of the chemistry regents is that the reference tables-based questions are the *easiest part of the regents by far* – **if you know how to use the reference tables.**

That's where this book comes in. ***Bonding with the Reference Tables: A Clear & Simple Chemistry Regents Guide*** is a book that:

- Gives step-by-step instructions in **clear** and **simple** terms on how to easily decipher each one of the 21 charts on the Chemistry Reference Tables

AND...

- Provides **actual regents questions** at the end of each section, along with answers and brief explanations at the end of the book

To Get the Most Out of This Book:

Read the book aloud with a friend so you don't miss anything important.

As you read through the book, follow along with a separate copy of the Chemistry Reference Tables. This way, you won't have to keep flipping pages from the tables to their explanations.

If you are pressed for time, start with the tables that appear most often on the regents. On each table, notice this icon with a number. This represents the average number of questions on that table per regents.

For example, on the **Table F: Solubility Guidelines** chart, you see . This means that there is approximately 1 question on this table per regents.

After you finish reading about each table, do the **practice regents questions** on the table to ensure you understood it correctly. The practice questions are conveniently included after each section, symbolized by this icon:

Note: Some regents questions have been edited slightly.

In addition, the "More Practice" section at the end of the book organizes all the reference tables-based regents questions from the January 2015-January 2020 regents by table.

These extra questions will provide you with even more opportunity to exercise the Reference Tables skills you have learned from this guide. This way, you will be fully prepared to tackle those questions on your upcoming regents exam.

Good luck!

Y. Finkel

Contents

NEW YORK STATE
CHEMISTRY REFERENCE TABLES

TABLE A

STANDARD TEMPERATURE & PRESSURE

Table A
Standard Temperature and Pressure

Name	Value	Unit
Standard Pressure	101.3 kPa 1 atm	kilopascal atmosphere
Standard Temperature	273 K 0°C	kelvin degree Celsius

1

TABLE A: Standard Temperature and Pressure

Table A Standard Temperature and Pressure		
Name	**Value**	**Unit**
Standard Pressure	101.3 kPa 1 atm	kilopascal atmosphere
Standard Temperature	273 K 0°C	kelvin degree Celsius

Table A gives you the values and units for standard pressure (i.e. air pressure at sea level) and standard temperature, otherwise known as *STP*.

Note: There are no single regents questions devoted specifically to Table A. This table simply provides you with information that can help you with other regents questions.

Reading the Table:

♦ This table is quite simple to use. Use it to look up *STP* – **Standard Temperature & Pressure** values whenever they're needed to solve a problem in conjunction with another table.

→ STP is used most often with:

⇨ Table S when figuring out the **phases** of different elements. (only standard temperature is used here)

✓ See **regents questions 11** and **16** in the Table S section.

⇨ Table T - the **Combined Gas Law** (both standard temperature and pressure used with this equation)

✓ See **regents questions 23** and **27** in the Table T section.

♦ Notice that both pressure and temperature are measured in *two units*: **Pressure** in **(kilo)pascals** and **atmospheres**, and *temperature* in **kelvins** and **degrees Celsius**.

→ This is important because when using Table A to look up either standard pressure or temperature to solve a given problem, you must use the same units as found in the problem, or you will get the wrong answer.

⇨ For example, using the **Combined Gas Law** on Table T, you may be given an original temperature in K and pressure in kPa, then asked to find the volume at STP.

✓ Technically, standard temperature could mean 273 K or 0°C, and standard pressure could mean 101.3 kPa or 1 atm. But since the problem uses K and kPa, use 273 K and 101.3 kPa to solve this problem.

NEW YORK STATE
CHEMISTRY REFERENCE TABLES

TABLE B

PHYSICAL CONSTANTS FOR WATER

Table B
Physical Constants for Water

Heat of Fusion	334 J/g
Heat of Vaporization	2260 J/g
Specific Heat Capacity of $H_2O(\ell)$	4.18 J/g•K

TABLE B: Physical Constants for Water

Table B
Physical Constants for Water

Heat of Fusion	334 J/g
Heat of Vaporization	2260 J/g
Specific Heat Capacity of $H_2O(\ell)$	4.18 J/g•K

Using the Table:

- On **Table T**, there are three **"Heat Equations"** written in symbols, with their keys to their immediate right. (*See clipping below.*)

- As seen clearly on the key, the *C* in the first heat equation, $q = mC\Delta T$, stands for the *specific heat capacity* of the liquid discussed.

  ➜ Since the liquid referenced is water unless stated otherwise, when solving this equation, use **Table B** to look up the **specific heat capacity of water**, which is **4.18 J/g·K** (4.18 Joules per gram times Kelvins), and substitute this value for the **"C"** in your equation.

Table B gives you three pieces of information (constants) about the *physical properties* of **water** that are used in conjunction with the three **heat equations** on **Table T** – Important Formulas and Equations.

➜ *Heat of fusion* → the amount of heat (measured in Joules) required to **melt** 1 gram of water at its melting point (0 °C)

➜ *Heat of vaporization* → the amount of heat (measured in Joules) required to **vaporize** (boil) 1 gram of water at its boiling point (100 °C)

➜ *Specific heat capacity* → the amount of heat required to **raise the temperature of 1 gram of water by 1 Kelvin**

Table T
Important Formulas and Equations

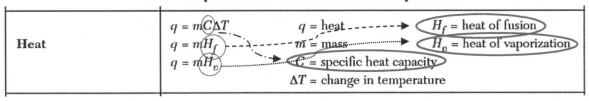

Heat	$q = mC\Delta T$	q = heat	H_f = heat of fusion
	$q = mH_f$	m = mass	H_v = heat of vaporization
	$q = mH_v$	C = specific heat capacity	
		ΔT = change in temperature	

⇨ How many joules of heat are absorbed when 50 g of H_2O are heated 28.4° C?

    ✓ $q = mC\varDelta T$; m = mass, C = specific heat capacity, $\varDelta T$ = change in temperature (on the key to the right of the equation on Table T)

    ✓ Given mass is 50 g – substitute 50 for m: $q = (50)C\varDelta T$

    ✓ Spec. heat cap. of H_2O is 4.18 J/g·K – substitute for C: $q = (50)(\mathbf{4.18})\varDelta T$

    ✓ Change in temp. is 28.4° C (same as 28.4 Kelvins) – substitute it for $\varDelta T$: $q = (50)(4.18)(28.4)$

    ✓ $q = 5935.6\,J$

⇨ How much heat is absorbed when 5 g of water are heated from 10° C to 20° C?

    ✓ $q = mC\varDelta T$

    ✓ q = (5)(**4.18**)(10)

    ✓ q = 209 J

♦ In the second and third heat equations, $\boldsymbol{q = mH_f}$ and $\boldsymbol{q = mH_v}$, H_f and H_v stand for *heat of fusion* and *heat of vaporization* respectively.

➔ Since the liquid referenced to by regents questions is always water, when solving either one of these equations, use Table B to look up the water's **heat of fusion** *(334 J/g)* or **heat of vaporization** *(2260 J/g)* and substitute these values into your equation.

  ⇨ How many joules are needed to melt 255 g of ice at 0° C?

    ✓ Since the question refers to *melting*, use the heat of fusion equation: $\boldsymbol{q = mH_f}$; m = mass, H_f = heat of fusion

    ✓ m = 255; $q = (255)H_f$

    ✓ H_f = 334; $q = (255)(\mathbf{334})$

    ✓ $q = 85170\,J$

  ⇨ How much heat is released when 10 g of H_2O freezes?

    ✓ Freezing is the opposite process of melting, so the same amount of energy is involved (it's released, though, not absorbed): use the heat of fusion equation again: $\boldsymbol{q = mH_f}$

    ✓ $q = (10)(\mathbf{334})$

    ✓ $q = 3340\,J$

⇨ How many joules are needed to *vaporize* 423 g of water at 100° C?

✓ Since the question refers to *vaporization*, use the heat of vaporization equation: $q = mH_v$; m = mass, H_v = heat of vaporization

✓ $m = 423$; $q = (423)H_v$

✓ $H_v = 2260$; $q = (423)(\mathbf{2260})$

✓ $q = 955,980\ J$

----

1. What is the amount of heat absorbed when the temperature of 75 grams of water increases from 20.°C to 35°C? *(Round your answer to the nearest whole number.)*

   (1) 1100 J   (3) 6300 J
   (2) 4700 J   (4) 11000 J

2. What is the amount of heat required to completely melt a 200.-gram sample of $H_2O(s)$ at STP?

   (1) 334 J   (3) 66800 J
   (2) 836 J   (4) 452000 J

3. Determine the quantity of heat released when 2.00 grams of H_2O (ℓ) freezes at 0°C.

4. Determine the total amount of heat, in joules, required to completely vaporize a 50.0-gram sample of H_2O (ℓ) at its boiling point at standard pressure.

5. Show a numerical setup *(show how you would set up an equation to solve but don't solve)* for calculating the quantity of heat in joules required to completely vaporize 102.3 grams of $H_2O(ℓ)$ at 100.°C and 1.0 atm.

NEW YORK STATE
CHEMISTRY REFERENCE TABLES

TABLES C & D

SELECTED PREFIXES
SELECTED UNITS

Table C
Selected Prefixes

Factor	Prefix	Symbol
10^3	kilo-	k
10^{-1}	deci-	d
10^{-2}	centi-	c
10^{-3}	milli-	m
10^{-6}	micro-	μ
10^{-9}	nano-	n
10^{-12}	pico-	p

Table D
Selected Units

Symbol	Name	Quantity
m	meter	length
g	gram	mass
Pa	pascal	pressure
K	kelvin	temperature
mol	mole	amount of substance
J	joule	energy, work, quantity of heat
s	second	time
min	minute	time
h	hour	time
d	day	time
y	year	time
L	liter	volume
ppm	parts per million	concentration
M	molarity	solution concentration
u	atomic mass unit	atomic mass

TABLES C & D: Selected Prefixes; Selected Units

Table C Selected Prefixes		
Factor	Prefix	Symbol
10^3	kilo-	k
10^{-1}	deci-	d
10^{-2}	centi-	c
10^{-3}	milli-	m
10^{-6}	micro-	μ
10^{-9}	nano-	n
10^{-12}	pico-	p

Table D Selected Units		
Symbol	Name	Quantity
m	meter	length
g	gram	mass
Pa	pascal	pressure
K	kelvin	temperature
mol	mole	amount of substance
J	joule	energy, work, quantity of heat
s	second	time
min	minute	time
h	hour	time
d	day	time
y	year	time
L	liter	volume
ppm	parts per million	concentration
M	molarity	solution concentration
u	atomic mass unit	atomic mass

> **Note:** There are very few single regents questions devoted specifically to Tables C or D. These tables simply provide you with information that can help you with other questions or help you understand other tables.

Reading the Tables:

♦ **Table C** lists common **prefixes** used in chemistry, their **symbols** and their **factors**. For example, the prefix *kilo-* is indicated by a *k* and means **1,000**. For example, a *kilo*gram means *1,000* **grams**, so 45 kg would equal 45,000 grams (45*1,000). Don't expect to consult this table too often. (It is likely that you won't use it at all.)

♦ **Table D** is more useful. It lists many **symbols** of selected units used on other tables and/or in regents questions and tells you what they **stand for** and what they **measure**.

→ For example, look at **Table B – Physical Constants for Water**. Table B says that Heat of Fusion is *334 J/g*. But what does *J* stand for? And what does *g* stand for? **Table D** tells you that J stands for **joule** and is a measure of energy/work/heat. G stands for gram and is a measure of mass. Now you can understand the table better!

→ Another example: Look at **Table N – Selected Radioisotopes**. In the **HALF-LIFE** column, you see symbols/abbreviations such as *s, min, h, d, y*. What do these stand for? **Table D** tells you that these are all units of time: s → seconds, min → minutes, h → hours, d → days, y → years.

NEW YORK STATE
CHEMISTRY REFERENCE TABLES

TABLE E

SELECTED POLYATOMIC IONS

Table E
Selected Polyatomic Ions

Formula	Name	Formula	Name
H_3O^+	hydronium	CrO_4^{2-}	chromate
Hg_2^{2+}	mercury(I)	$Cr_2O_7^{2-}$	dichromate
NH_4^+	ammonium	MnO_4^-	permanganate
$C_2H_3O_2^-$ CH_3COO^- }	acetate	NO_2^-	nitrite
		NO_3^-	nitrate
CN^-	cyanide	O_2^{2-}	peroxide
CO_3^{2-}	carbonate	OH^-	hydroxide
HCO_3^-	hydrogen carbonate	PO_4^{3-}	phosphate
$C_2O_4^{2-}$	oxalate	SCN^-	thiocyanate
ClO^-	hypochlorite	SO_3^{2-}	sulfite
ClO_2^-	chlorite	SO_4^{2-}	sulfate
ClO_3^-	chlorate	HSO_4^-	hydrogen sulfate
ClO_4^-	perchlorate	$S_2O_3^{2-}$	thiosulfate

TABLE E: Selected Polyatomic Ions

Table E
Selected Polyatomic Ions

Formula	Name	Formula	Name
H_3O^+	hydronium	CrO_4^{2-}	chromate
Hg_2^{2+}	mercury(I)	$Cr_2O_7^{2-}$	dichromate
NH_4^+	ammonium	MnO_4^-	permanganate
$C_2H_3O_2^-$ }CH_3COO^- }	acetate	NO_2^-	nitrite
		NO_3^-	nitrate
CN^-	cyanide	O_2^{2-}	peroxide
CO_3^{2-}	carbonate	OH^-	hydroxide
HCO_3^-	hydrogen carbonate	PO_4^{3-}	phosphate
$C_2O_4^{2-}$	oxalate	SCN^-	thiocyanate
ClO^-	hypochlorite	SO_3^{2-}	sulfite
ClO_2^-	chlorite	SO_4^{2-}	sulfate
ClO_3^-	chlorate	HSO_4^-	hydrogen sulfate
ClO_4^-	perchlorate	$S_2O_3^{2-}$	thiosulfate

Table E contains the names and formulas of 25 different **polyatomic ions**.

Polyatomic ion → several atoms covalently bonded resulting in a **charged particle** – an **ion**. Compounds with polyatomic ions within their structures are both **ionically** and **covalently** bonded.

Covalent bond → a relatively weak chemical bond created when an atom **shares** its valence electrons with another atom (or atoms)

Ionic bond → a stronger chemical bond created when valence electrons are **transferred** from one atom to another.

Table E is helpful...

→ For **identifying** polyatomic ions *within formulas*

→ When **writing formulas** of compounds containing polyatomic ions

Reading the Table:

- The **FORMULA** column tells you which elements make up each polyatomic ion, using the element's symbol, and how many of that element using subscripts.

    → Notice the **charge** in the upper right corner of each polyatomic ion. The charge is not just for the last element of the polyatomic ion – it is the *entire polyatomic ion* that is charged. It is this charge that gives it its ionic status and enable it to bond with other (regular) ions. (See below for further explanation.)

    → A charge of "+" or "-" without a number is understood to be "**+1**" or "**-1**."

- The **NAME** column gives you the chemical name of each polyatomic ion listed. Notice that many polyatomic ions end in "**–ate**."

- <u>Common Regents Questions on Table E:</u>

    → Often, you are asked to identify the polyatomic ion within a formula or a group of formulas. To answer these kinds of questions, simply look through **Table E**. If part of the formula is on Table E, that part is a polyatomic ion.

⇨ **Ex1:** Within the formula of potassium phosphate (K_3PO_4), the phosphate – PO_4 is the polyatomic ion.

⇨ **Ex2:** Within the formula of magnesium chlorate: $Mg(ClO_3)_2$, the chlorate – ClO_3 is the polyatomic ion. (The subscript 2 outside the parenthesis in magnesium chlorate's formula tells you that there are 2 chlorates present.)

→ If you are given a compound containing a polyatomic ion (any formula on **Table E**), such as Na_2**CO_3** (containing the polyatomic ion **carbonate**) and asked which two types of chemical bonding are contained within this compound, the answer will always be **"ionic and covalent."** (This is because while the atoms that make up a polyatomic ion are covalently bonded – the elements are sharing valence electrons with each other, the polyatomic ion has a charge, which attracts and attaches to another ion of an opposite charge. This is ionic bonding.)

⇨ The same is true vice versa. If asked to choose the compound that contains more than one kind of chemical bonding, look for a **polyatomic ion** from **Table E**.

→ If asked where the ionic bond is in a compound containing a polyatomic ion, such as K_3**PO_4**, it is between the *entire polyatomic ion* (PO_4) and the *other element* in the compound (K). Do not split up the ion and choose K_3P and O_4 as your answer, since the entire PO_4 makes up the ion.

→ To ***write the formula*** of a compound containing a polyatomic ion, follow the regular steps (discussed under **oxidation states** in the **PT**), but treat the entire ion as a single unit, with the charge belonging to the whole thing.

⇨ <u>Example 1:</u> What is the chemical formula for ***ammonium*** *sulfide*?

✓ Write out the symbols of each element/polyatomic ion with their oxidation states (charges): **$(NH_4)^+S^{2-}$**

✓ "Crisscross" each charge, changing it to a subscript of the other element. Omit the charges: **$(NH_4)_2S_1$** - notice the charge from the S became a subscript of the entire NH_4, indicated by the parenthesis around the ion.

✓ If one subscript is a factor of another, simplify. If any of the subscripts is a 1, leave it out: **$(NH_4)_2S$**

⇨ <u>Example 2:</u> What is the chemical formula for *magnesium **nitrate***?

✓ Write out the symbols with their oxidation states: **$Mg^{2+}(NO_3)^-$**

✓ "Crisscross" each charge, changing it to a subscript. Omit the charges: **$Mg_1(NO_3)_2$**

✓ Simplify: **$Mg(NO_3)_2$**

1. Which polyatomic ion is found in the compound represented by the formula $NaHCO_3$?
   (1) hydrogen sulfate
   (2) hydrogen carbonate
   (3) Acetate
   (4) oxalate

2. Which polyatomic ion has a charge of 3-?
   (1) chromate   (3) phosphate
   (2) oxalate   (4) thiocyanate

3. What is the name of the polyatomic ion in the compound Na_2O_2?
   (1) Hydroxide   (3) oxide
   (2) Oxalate   (4) peroxide

4. What is the chemical formula for ammonium sulfide?
   (1) $(NH_4)_2S$ (3) $(NH_4)_2SO_4$
   (2) $(NH_4)_2SO_3$ (4) $(NH_4)_2S_2O_3$

5. What is the chemical formula for sodium sulfate?
   (1) Na_2SO_4 (3) $NaSO_4$
   (2) Na_2SO_3 (4) $NaSO_3$

6. What is the chemical formula for zinc carbonate?
   (1) $ZnCO_3$ (3) Zn_2CO_3
   (2) $Zn(CO_3)_2$ (4) Zn_3CO

7. In the compound $KHSO_4$, there is an ionic bond between the
   (1) KH^+ and SO_4^{2-} ions
   (2) $KHSO_3^-$ and O^{2-} ions
   (3) K^+ and HS^- ions
   (4) K^+ and HSO_4^- ions

8. Magnesium nitrate contains chemical bonds that are
   (1) covalent, only
   (2) ionic, only
   (3) both covalent and ionic
   (4) neither covalent nor ionic

9. Which compound contains both ionic and covalent bonds?
   (1) Ammonia
   (2) sodium nitrate
   (3) methane
   (4) potassium chloride

10. *Thermal energy is absorbed as chemical reactions occur during the process of baking muffins. The batter for muffins often contains baking soda, $NaHCO_3(s)$, which decomposes as the muffins are baked in an oven at 200.°C...*
    $2NaHCO_3(s) + heat \rightarrow Na_2CO_3(s) + H_2O(\ell) + CO_2(g)$
    Based on Table E, identify the polyatomic ion in the solid product of the reaction.

11. *Potassium phosphate, K_3PO_4, is a source of dietary potassium found in a popular cereal...*
    Identify two types of chemical bonding in the source of dietary potassium in this cereal.

12. Identify both types of bonds in $NH_4NO_3(s)$.

NEW YORK STATE
CHEMISTRY REFERENCE TABLES

TABLE F

SOLUBILITY GUIDELINES FOR AQUEOUS SOLUTIONS

Table F
Solubility Guidelines for Aqueous Solutions

Ions That Form *Soluble* Compounds	Exceptions	Ions That Form *Insoluble* Compounds*	Exceptions
Group 1 ions (Li$^+$, Na$^+$, etc.)		carbonate (CO$_3^{2-}$)	when combined with Group 1 ions or ammonium (NH$_4^+$)
ammonium (NH$_4^+$)		chromate (CrO$_4^{2-}$)	when combined with Group 1 ions, Ca^{2+}, Mg^{2+}, or ammonium (NH$_4^+$)
nitrate (NO$_3^-$)			
acetate (C$_2$H$_3$O$_2^-$ or CH$_3$COO$^-$)		phosphate (PO$_4^{3-}$)	when combined with Group 1 ions or ammonium (NH$_4^+$)
hydrogen carbonate (HCO$_3^-$)		sulfide (S^{2-})	when combined with Group 1 ions or ammonium (NH$_4^+$)
chlorate (ClO$_3^-$)		hydroxide (OH$^-$)	when combined with Group 1 ions, Ca^{2+}, Ba^{2+}, Sr^{2+}, or ammonium (NH$_4^+$)
halides (Cl$^-$, Br$^-$, I$^-$)	when combined with Ag$^+$, Pb^{2+}, or Hg$_2^{2+}$		
sulfates (SO$_4^{2-}$)	when combined with Ag$^+$, Ca^{2+}, Sr^{2+}, Ba^{2+}, or Pb^{2+}	*compounds having very low solubility in H$_2$O	

TABLE F: Solubility Guidelines for Aqueous Solutions

Table F
Solubility Guidelines for Aqueous Solutions

Ions That Form *Soluble* Compounds	Exceptions	Ions That Form *Insoluble* Compounds*	Exceptions
Group 1 ions (Li^+, Na^+, etc.)		carbonate (CO_3^{2-})	when combined with Group 1 ions or ammonium (NH_4^+)
ammonium (NH_4^+)		chromate (CrO_4^{2-})	when combined with Group 1 ions, Ca^{2+}, Mg^{2+}, or ammonium (NH_4^+)
nitrate (NO_3^-)			
acetate ($C_2H_3O_2^-$ or CH_3COO^-)		phosphate (PO_4^{3-})	when combined with Group 1 ions or ammonium (NH_4^+)
hydrogen carbonate (HCO_3^-)		sulfide (S^{2-})	when combined with Group 1 ions or ammonium (NH_4^+)
chlorate (ClO_3^-)		hydroxide (OH^-)	when combined with Group 1 ions, Ca^{2+}, Ba^{2+}, Sr^{2+}, or ammonium (NH_4^+)
halides (Cl^-, Br^-, I^-)	when combined with Ag^+, Pb^{2+}, or Hg_2^{2+}		
sulfates (SO_4^{2-})	when combined with Ag^+, Ca^{2+}, Sr^{2+}, Ba^{2+}, or Pb^{2+}	*compounds having very low solubility in H_2O	

Reading the Table:

♦ The *first* half of the table (left side) lists **IONS THAT** [usually] **FORM SOLUBLE COMPOUNDS**. **EXCEPTIONS** are listed to the immediate right of this column. If an ion is listed under the exceptions, it is either not soluble at all – *insoluble* – or it is *slightly* soluble.

  → Ex: *Group 1 ions*, such as **Li⁺** and **Na⁺**, are *always soluble* in water, since there are *no exceptions* listed.

    ⇒ **NaCl** is *always* soluble in water, since it includes *Na⁺*, which is always soluble, in its composition.

    ⇒ **NOTE:** Li⁺ and Na⁺ are only *examples* of group 1 ions. There are more ions included in this category, such as K⁺ and Rb⁺. *See the* **PT** *for the full list.*

Table F lists different ions and their *solubility levels* in aqueous (water-based) solutions. Based on the information in the table, it is possible to figure out whether or a not a specific compound (composed of more than one ion) is soluble in water or not.

Solubility → how well a substance will dissolve into another substance:

  → *Soluble compound* → dissolves well – also known as an **"electrolyte"** (because it conducts electricity when dissolved)

  → *Insoluble compound* → does not dissolve well – also known as a **"precipitate"**

➔ <u>Ex:</u> *Halides* (Group 17 ions) such as **Cl⁻**, are usually soluble in water, *except* when they are combined with either **Ag⁺, Pb²⁺** or **Hg₂²⁺**.

⇨ **PbBr₂** is *in*soluble, since it contains a Pb²⁺ ion. (When the ion is part of a compound, its charge is not included. Just look for the elements that make up the ion without the charge.)

⇨ **NOTE:** You often must determine the solubility of a compound given its name in *words*, (i.e. **lead sulfate**), not *symbols* (i.e. **PbSO₄**). *Use the* PT *and* Table S *to* check what unfamiliar symbols mean. (*Ag* – silver, *Pb* – lead, *Hg* – mercury, etc.)

♦ The *second* half of the table (right side) lists **IONS THAT FORM *INSOLUBLE* COMPOUNDS**, unless they are combined with any of the **EXCEPTIONS** listed to their right. If an ion is listed under the exceptions here, that means it *is* soluble.

➔ <u>Ex:</u> A compound containing **carbonate (CO₃²⁻)** is insoluble *unless it also contains a* **Group 1 ion** *or* **ammonium** (which are listed as *always soluble* with no exceptions).

⇨ **MgS** is insoluble because it contains sulfide (a sulfur ion) and does not contain a Group 1 ion or ammonium.

⇨ **Note:** as seen in the **EXCEPTIONS** column, all insoluble ions listed become soluble when combined with Group 1 ions or ammonium. *Chromate* and *hydroxide* also have other exceptions besides these two.

♦ Instead of simply asking, "Which compound is soluble/insoluble in water," the regents often phrases multiple choice questions on this table as follows: *"Which compound is **most/least** soluble?"* To answer either form of this question:

➔ For "*most* soluble," simply determine which of the four choices you are given is *soluble*. The other choices will be insoluble.

➔ For "*least* soluble," just find the one choice that is *insoluble*. The other choices will be soluble.

♦ To use the table to *determine the solubility of a given compound*, look for either part of the compound on the table:

➔ If one part is in the *soluble* column, this means that the compound is *soluble*, unless the other part of the compound is *among the exceptions* listed.

➔ The same is true if one part is listed in the *insoluble* column. It is *insoluble*, unless the other half of the compound is listed as an exception for this ion.

Examples:

1. Is *AgBr* soluble in water?

→ It would seem so at first glance, since Br^- is listed as an ion that forms a soluble compound. However, notice that since the Br^- is combined with Ag^+, an exception, it is not soluble, or *insoluble.*

2. Is *CaCO₃* soluble in water?

→ CO_3^{2-} is classified as an insoluble ion. Since Ca^+ is not among the exceptions (it's a Group *2* ion, not a Group 1 ion), the compound remains *insoluble*.

3. Is *(NH₄)₂S* soluble in water?

→ NH_4^+ is soluble, with no exceptions. So, the compound is **soluble**. (Alternatively, you could have found S^{2-} listed as an insoluble compound unless combined with Group 1 ions or *ammonium – NH_4^+*.)

4. Is *Li₂CO₃* soluble in water?

→ Lithium (Li^+) is a Group 1 ion, which is always soluble, with no exceptions. So, the compound is **soluble**. (Alternatively, you could have found CO_3^{2-} listed as an insoluble compound unless combined with *Group 1 ions* or ammonium – NH_4^+.)

1. *A bottled water label lists the ions dissolved in the water. The table to the right lists the mass of some ions dissolved in a 500.-gram sample of the bottled water.* Based on Table F, write the formula of the ion in the bottled water table that would form the *least* soluble compound when combined with the sulfate ion.

Ions in 500. g of Bottled Water

Ion Formula	Mass (g)
Ca^{2+}	0.040
Mg^{2+}	0.013
Na^+	0.0033
SO_4^{2-}	0.0063
HCO_3^-	0.180

2. *Some compounds of silver are listed with their chemical formulas in the table to the right.* Identify the silver compound in the table that is most soluble in water.

Silver Compounds

Name	Chemical Formula
silver carbonate	Ag_2CO_3
silver chlorate	$AgClO_3$
silver chloride	$AgCl$
silver sulfate	Ag_2SO_4

3. Based on Table F, identify one ion that reacts with iodide ions in an aqueous solution to form an insoluble compound.

4. Based on Table F, which equation represents a saturated solution having the lowest concentration of Cl⁻ ions? [In other words, "Which equation contains a compound that is least soluble – doesn't dissolve well, producing the fewest Cl⁻ ions?"]

(1) $NaCl(s) \rightleftharpoons Na^+(aq) + Cl^-(aq)$

(2) $AgCl(s) \rightleftharpoons Ag^+(aq) + Cl^-(aq)$

(3) $NH_4Cl(s) \rightleftharpoons NH_4^+(aq) + Cl^-(aq)$

(4) $KCl(s) \rightleftharpoons K^+(aq) + Cl^-(aq)$

5. According to Table F, which substance is *most* soluble in water?
   (1) AgCl   (3) Na_2CO_3
   (2) $CaCO_3$ (4) $SrSO_4$

6. Based on Table F, which compound is *least* soluble in water?
   (1) $AlPO_4$ (3) Li_2SO_4
   (2) $Ca(OH)_2$ (4) $AgC_2H_3O_2$

7. According to Table *F*, which ions combine with chloride ions to form an insoluble compound?
   (1) Fe₂_ ions   (3) Li_ ions
   (2) Ca₂_ ions   (4) Ag_ ions

My Notes on the Previous Section(s):

_____

_____

_____

_____

_____

_____

_____

_____

_____

_____

_____

_____

_____

_____

_____

_____

_____

_____

_____

_____

_____

_____

_____

_____

_____

_____

New York State
Chemistry Reference Tables

Table G

Solubility Curves at Standard Pressure

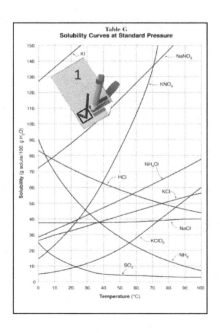

TABLE G: Solubility Curves at Standard Pressure

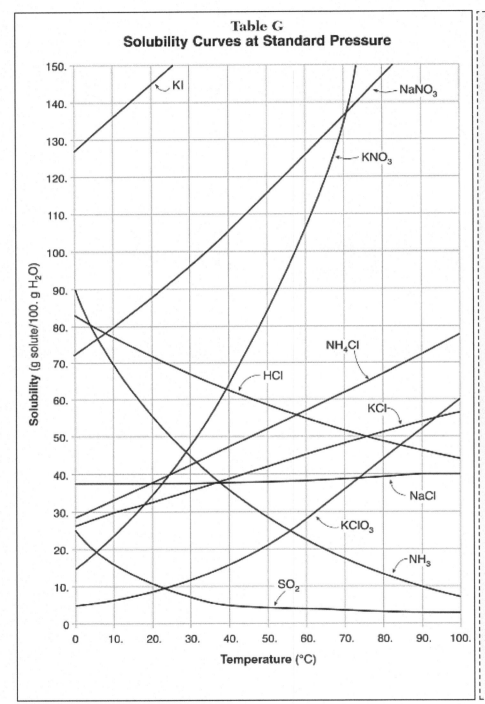

Table G is a graph that gives you the **solubility trend** for ten common substances (how much of that substance will dissolve in water) based on **temperature variations**:

→ For **solid** and **liquid** solutes, as temperature *increases*, solubility *increase*s.

→ For **gas** solutes, as temperature *increases*, solubility *decrease*s.

You can also use the table to determine **saturation levels** of given solutions.

→ **Saturated solution** → a solution that is *filled to capacity* – it is holding (dissolved within it) the exact amount of solute it can hold.

→ **Unsaturated solution** → a solution that is *not full*. It is still capable of dissolving more solute.

Reading the Table:

• <u>Basic points about the graph:</u>

➔ The **horizontal axis** represents the **TEMPERATURE**, measured in *degrees Celsius (°C)*. It ranges from 0 degrees to 100 degrees, with a scale of ten.

➔ The **vertical axis** represents the **SOLUBILITY**, measured in *grams of solute per one hundred grams of water (g solute/100. g H_2O)*. It ranges from 0 grams to 150 grams, also with a scale of ten.

➔ Each **dark labeled curve** on the graph represents a different compound. The seven curves sloping in an *upwards* direction [L → R] represent *solid* compounds, while the three curves sloping *downwards* represent *gaseous* compounds. (Because temperature has opposite effects on the solubility of solids and gases. See gray box on previous page.)

• <u>Reading the graph:</u>

➔ Read *up* from the **TEMPERATURE** on the x-axis to the line labeled with the appropriate formula (or substance) and then to the *left* for the number of grams to make a saturated solution. The line represents a saturated solution for that formula at various temperatures.

➔ The point where the temperature and solubility axis meet a curve tells you how many grams of this compound 100 grams of water can hold at this temperature. In other words, it gives you a solution made of that specific compound's *saturation level* at that temperature.

⇨ <u>Ex</u>: At **20°C**, a solution of 100 g of water can hold approximately **145 g** of **KI** [top left]. In other words, a solution of KI is *saturated* with 145 g at 20°C.

⇨ <u>Ex</u>: At **70°C**, a solution of 100 g of water can hold approximately **18 g** of **NH₃** [bottom right]. In other words, a solution of NH_3 is *saturated* with 18 g at 70°C.

⇨ <u>Ex</u>: At **30°C**, a solution of 100 g of water can hold approximately **67 g** of **HCl** [middle]. In other words, a solution of HCl is *saturated* with 67 g at 30°C.

➔ If the point where the temperature (ex: **80°C**) and the number of grams – solubility (ex: **60 g**) meet is *below* that formula's curve, this means that a solution of this compound is *unsaturated* at this temperature. The solution would still be able to dissolve more solute.

⇨ <u>Ex</u>: A solution of 100 grams of water and **60 g** of **NH₄Cl** [middle right] at **80°C** is *unsaturated*, since at 80°C, the solution should be able to hold approximately 67 g of NH_4Cl, not just 60 g.

⇨ <u>Ex:</u> A solution of 100 grams of water and **110 g** of **KNO₃** [top right] at **70°C** is *unsaturated*, since at 70°C, the solution should be able to hold approximately 133 g of NH₄Cl, not just 110 g.

→ Sometimes, you are asked how many more grams of solute a solution needs to become saturated at a specific temperature. To figure this out, simply **subtract** *the amount of solute currently dissolved* in the solution from *the amount of solute the solution can hold* when saturated.

⇨ <u>Ex:</u> At **30°C**, **25.0** grams of **KCl**(s) are dissolved in 100. grams of $H_2O(l)$. Based on Table G, determine the additional mass of KCl(s) that must be dissolved to saturate the solution at 30°C.

✓ **Key:** At 30°C, the solution of KCl can hold about **35** g of solute. Currently, it only has 25 g. Subtract: $35 - 25 = $ **10**. *10 g of KCl must be dissolved to saturate the solution at 30°C.*

→ **Note:** As you may have noticed, every problem we've worked with so far used *100 grams* of water as the amount of solvent (substance that is dissolving) in the solution. This is because that is the way **SOLUBILITY** is measured on this table: g of solvent per 100 grams of water. *However, the regents can present an example using only 50 grams of water, or sometimes 200 grams of water.* <u>Why is this important?</u>

⇨ If there are only *50 g* of water, the solution can only hold **half** of the amount of solute the graph seems to indicate that it can hold at this temperature, because there is only half the amount of solvent available to dissolve the solute.

✓ <u>Ex:</u> At **90°C**, a solution of **50 g** of water is saturated with **20 g** of **NaCl** [bottom right] – half of 40 g.

✓ <u>Ex:</u> At **40°C**, a solution of **50 g** of water is saturated with **2.5 g** of **SO₂** [bottom middle] – half of 5 g.

⇨ If there are *200 g* of water, the solution can hold **double** the amount of solute than the graph seems to indicate, because there is double the amount of solvent available.

✓ <u>Ex:</u> At **10°C**, a solution of **200 g** of water is still *un*saturated with **100 g** of **NH₃** [bottom right], since it can hold 140 g – double 70 g – of NH₃ at this temperature.

✓ <u>Ex:</u> At **30°C**, a solution of **200 g** of water is saturated at approximately **84 g** of **NH₄Cl** [middle right].

1. *At 23°C, 85.0 grams of NaNO₃(s) are dissolved in 100. grams of H₂O(l̸).* Based on Table G, determine the additional mass of NaNO₃(s) that must be dissolved to saturate the solution at 23°C.

2. *In a laboratory investigation, a student is given a sample that is a mixture of 3.0 grams of NaCl(s) and 4.0 grams of sand, which is mostly SiO₂(s). The purpose of the investigation is to separate and recover the compounds in the sample. In the first step, the student places the sample in a 250-mL flask. Then, **50.** grams of distilled water are added to the flask, and the contents are thoroughly stirred. The mixture in the flask is then filtered, using the equipment represented by the diagram below.*

Based on Table G, state evidence that all the NaCl(s) in the flask would dissolve in the distilled water at 20.°C.

Questions 3 & 4: *A saturated solution of sulfur dioxide is prepared by dissolving SO₂(g) in 100. grams of water at 10.°C and standard pressure.*

3. Determine the mass of SO₂ in this solution.

4. Based on Table G, state the general relationship between solubility and temperature of an aqueous SO₂ solution at standard pressure.

5. According to Table G, which substance forms an unsaturated solution when 80. grams of the substance are stirred into 100. grams of H₂O at 10.°C?
   (1) KNO₃   (3) KI
   (2) NH₃   (4) NaCl

6. *A solution is made by dissolving 70.0 grams of KNO₃(s) in 100. grams of water at 50.°C and standard pressure.* Determine the number of additional grams of KNO₃ that must dissolve to make this solution saturated.

My Notes on the Previous Section(s):

_____

_____

_____

_____

_____

_____

_____

_____

_____

_____

_____

_____

_____

_____

_____

_____

_____

_____

_____

_____

_____

_____

_____

NEW YORK STATE
CHEMISTRY REFERENCE TABLES

TABLE H

VAPOR PRESSURE OF FOUR LIQUIDS

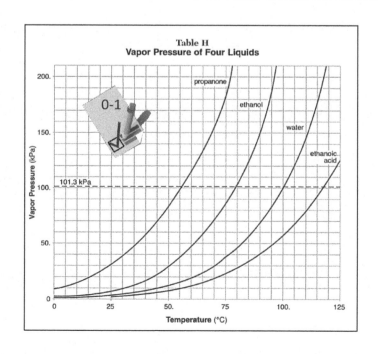

Table H
Vapor Pressure of Four Liquids

TABLE H: Vapor Pressure of Four Liquids

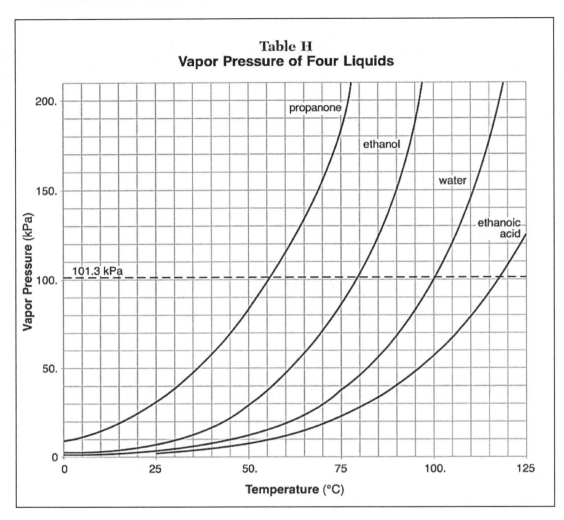

Table H
Vapor Pressure of Four Liquids

Table H is a graph with four curves representing four common liquids. It shows you the *relationship between* **temperature** *and* **vapor pressure** for these liquids. The graph also indicates **standard pressure, 101.3 kPa**, with a horizontal dashed line across the graph, which is sometimes used to find a liquid's **boiling point**.

Vapor pressure → the pressure exerted by evaporating liquids onto the surface of the liquid below (from where it evaporated) and onto the sides of its container, measured in **kilopascals** (kPa). As seen on the graph, the higher the temperature, the higher the vapor pressure, because higher temperatures lead to more liquid evaporating.

Boiling point → the temperature at which the *atmospheric (outside) pressure on a liquid's surface is equal to the liquid's vapor pressure*

Reading the Table:

♦ <u>Basic points about the graph:</u>

➔ The **horizontal axis** represents the **TEMPERATURE**, measured in *degrees Celsius (°C)*. It ranges from 0 degrees to 125 degrees, with a scale of five.

➔ The **vertical axis** represents the **VAPOR PRESSURE**, measured in *kilopascals (kPa)*. It ranges from 0 kPa to 210 kPa, with a scale of ten.

➔ Each **dark labeled curve** on the graph represents a different liquid.

➔ The **horizontal dashed line** labeled **101.3 kPa** is equivalent to *standard pressure*. It helps you find the **boiling point** of a substance.

♦ <u>Reading the graph:</u>

➔ Read *up* from the **TEMPERATURE** to the curve line labeled with the appropriate name and then to the *left* to the **VAPOR PRESSURE**.

➔ The point where the **TEMPERATURE** and **VAPOR PRESSURE** axis meet a curve gives you that liquid's vapor pressure at that specific temperature.

⇨ <u>Ex:</u> What is **ethanoic acid**'s *vapor pressure* at **90°C**? Approx. **40 kPa**.

⇨ <u>Ex:</u> At which *temperature* will **ethanol** have a vapor pressure of **30 kPa**? **50° C**

➔ To find a liquid's ***boiling point*** at *any atmospheric pressure*, find the given atmospheric pressure on the **VAPOR PRESSURE** axis (because when a liquid is at its boiling point, vapor pressure is equal to atmospheric pressure) and move to right until you hit that liquid's **curve**. Then move down and see where it hits the **TEMPERATURE** axis.

⇨ <u>Ex:</u> What is the boiling point of **ethanoic acid** if the pressure on its surface is **40 kPa**? **90°C**

⇨ <u>Ex:</u> At an atmospheric pressure of **145 kPa**, what's the boiling point of water? **110°C**

➔ To find a liquid's ***boiling point*** at *standard pressure* (101.3 kPa/1 atm), find the point where that liquid's curve meets the (dashed) horizontal line labeled 101.3 kPa. Then move down to the **TEMPERATURE** axis. (Because if a liquid is at its boiling point at standard pressure, its vapor pressure must be 101.3 kPa – equal to standard pressure. See gray box above.)

⇨ <u>Ex:</u> At standard pressure, what's water's boiling point? **100°C**

⇨ Ex: What's propanone's boiling point at standard pressure? Approx. **57°C**

→ Sometimes, the regents will refer to the liquids on this graph by their *structural formulas* – not their standard IUPAC ("official") name. For example, **ethanoic acid** can be referred to as **CH₃COOH (aq)**. Use Table R: Organic Functional Groups to help you figure out which liquid the question is referring to. (Ethanoic acid's formula can also be found on Table K: Common Acids.)

- -

1. What is the vapor pressure of propanone at 50.°C?
   (1) 37 kPa   (3) 50. kPa
   (2) 83 kPa   (4) 101 kPa

2. At which temperature is the vapor pressure of ethanol equal to 80. kPa?
   (1) 48°C   (3) 80.°C
   (2) 73°C   (4) 101°C

3. Which compound has the lowest vapor pressure at 50°C?
   (1) ethanoic acid   (3) propanone
   (2) ethanol   (4) water

4. *The boiling point of a liquid is the temperature at which the vapor pressure of the liquid is equal to the pressure on the surface of the liquid.* What is the boiling point of propanone if the pressure on its surface is 48 kilopascals?
   (1) 25°C   (3) 35°C
   (2) 30.°C   (4) 40.°C

5. At 65°C, which compound has a vapor pressure of 58 kilopascals?
   (1) ethanoic acid   (3) propanone
   (2) ethanol   (4) water

6. At which temperature is the vapor pressure of ethanol equal to the vapor pressure of propanone at 35°C?
   (1) 35°C   (3) 82°C
   (2) 60.°C   (4) 95°C

7. *A liquid's boiling point is the temperature at which its vapor pressure is equal to the atmospheric pressure.* Using Reference Table H, what is the boiling point of propanone at an atmospheric pressure of 70 kPa?

8. *Rubbing alcohol is a product available at most pharmacies and supermarkets. One rubbing alcohol solution contains 2-propanol and water. The boiling point of 2-propanol is 82.3°C at standard pressure. Determine the vapor pressure of water at a temperature equal to the boiling point of the 2-propanol.*

NEW YORK STATE
CHEMISTRY REFERENCE TABLES

TABLE I

HEATS OF REACTION AT 101.3 KPA & 298 K

Table I
Heats of Reaction at 101.3 kPa and 298 K

Reaction	ΔH (kJ)*
$CH_4(g) + 2O_2(g) \longrightarrow CO_2(g) + 2H_2O(\ell)$	–890.4
$C_3H_8 + 5O_2(g) \longrightarrow 3CO_2(g) + 4H_2O(\ell)$	–2219.2
$2C_8H_{18} + 25O_2(g) \longrightarrow 16CO_2(g) + 18H_2O(\ell)$	–10943
$2CO_2(g) + 4H_2O(\ell)$	–1452
$2CO_2(g) + 3H_2O(\ell)$	–1367
$C_6H_{12}O_6 \longrightarrow 6CO_2(g) + 6H_2O(\ell)$	–2804
$2CO(g) + O_2 \longrightarrow 2CO_2(g)$	–566.0
$C(s) + O_2 \longrightarrow CO_2(g)$	–393.5
$4Al(s) + 3O_2(g) \longrightarrow 2Al_2O_3(s)$	–3351
$N_2(g) + O_2(g) \longrightarrow 2NO(g)$	+182.6
$N_2(g) + 2O_2(g) \longrightarrow 2NO_2(g)$	+66.4
$2H_2(g) + O_2(g) \longrightarrow 2H_2O(g)$	–483.6
$2H_2(g) + O_2(g) \longrightarrow 2H_2O(\ell)$	–571.6
$N_2(g) + 3H_2(g) \longrightarrow 2NH_3(g)$	–91.8
$2C(s) + 3H_2(g) \longrightarrow C_2H_6(g)$	–84.0
$2C(s) + 2H_2(g) \longrightarrow C_2H_4(g)$	+52.4
$2C(s) + H_2(g) \longrightarrow C_2H_2(g)$	+227.4
$H_2(g) + I_2(g) \longrightarrow 2HI(g)$	+53.0
$KNO_3(s) \xrightarrow{H_2O} K^+(aq) + NO_3^-(aq)$	+34.89
$NaOH(s) \xrightarrow{H_2O} Na^+(aq) + OH^-(aq)$	–44.51
$NH_4Cl(s) \xrightarrow{H_2O} NH_4^+(aq) + Cl^-(aq)$	+14.78
$NH_4NO_3(s) \xrightarrow{H_2O} NH_4^+(aq) + NO_3^-(aq)$	+25.69
$NaCl(s) \xrightarrow{H_2O} Na^+(aq) + Cl^-(aq)$	+3.58
$LiBr(s) \xrightarrow{H_2O} Li^+(aq) + Br^-(aq)$	–48.83
$H^+(aq) + OH^-(aq) \longrightarrow H_2O(\ell)$	–55.8

*The ΔH values are based on molar quantities represented in the equations.
A minus sign indicates an exothermic reaction.

0-1

TABLE I: Heats of Reaction at 101.3 kPa & 298 K

Table I lists *many common chemical reactions*, along with their **delta H (ΔH)** values, measured in *kilojoules (kJ)*.

The symbol **delta** (Δ) means *change in*.

$\Delta H \rightarrow$ a measurement of *how much energy was absorbed or released* during the reaction. **Endothermic** reactions have positive ΔHs, while **exothermic** reactions have negative ΔHs.

Endothermic reaction

$\rightarrow$ a reaction that involves the **absorption** of heat:

➜ *Products* have more energy than *the reactants*.

➜ Energy is on the *left* (reactant) side of the chemical equation.

➜ ΔH is positive.

Exothermic reaction $\rightarrow$ a

reaction that involves the **release** of heat:

➜ *Products* have less energy than the *reactants*.

➜ Energy is on the *right* (product) side of the chemical equation.

➜ ΔH is negative.

Table I
Heats of Reaction at 101.3 kPa and 298 K

Reaction	ΔH (kJ)*
$CH_4(g) + 2O_2(g) \longrightarrow CO_2(g) + 2H_2O(\ell)$	–890.4
$C_3H_8(g) + 5O_2(g) \longrightarrow 3CO_2(g) + 4H_2O(\ell)$	–2219.2
$2C_8H_{18}(\ell) + 25O_2(g) \longrightarrow 16CO_2(g) + 18H_2O(\ell)$	–10943
$2CH_3OH(\ell) + 3O_2(g) \longrightarrow 2CO_2(g) + 4H_2O(\ell)$	–1452
$C_2H_5OH(\ell) + 3O_2(g) \longrightarrow 2CO_2(g) + 3H_2O(\ell)$	–1367
$C_6H_{12}O_6(s) + 6O_2(g) \longrightarrow 6CO_2(g) + 6H_2O(\ell)$	–2804
$2CO(g) + O_2(g) \longrightarrow 2CO_2(g)$	–566.0
$C(s) + O_2(g) \longrightarrow CO_2(g)$	–393.5
$4Al(s) + 3O_2(g) \longrightarrow 2Al_2O_3(s)$	–3351
$N_2(g) + O_2(g) \longrightarrow 2NO(g)$	+182.6
$N_2(g) + 2O_2(g) \longrightarrow 2NO_2(g)$	+66.4
$2H_2(g) + O_2(g) \longrightarrow 2H_2O(g)$	–483.6
$2H_2(g) + O_2(g) \longrightarrow 2H_2O(\ell)$	–571.6
$N_2(g) + 3H_2(g) \longrightarrow 2NH_3(g)$	–91.8
$2C(s) + 3H_2(g) \longrightarrow C_2H_6(g)$	–84.0
$2C(s) + 2H_2(g) \longrightarrow C_2H_4(g)$	+52.4
$2C(s) + H_2(g) \longrightarrow C_2H_2(g)$	+227.4
$H_2(g) + I_2(g) \longrightarrow 2HI(g)$	+53.0
$KNO_3(s) \xrightarrow{H_2O} K^+(aq) + NO_3^-(aq)$	+34.89
$NaOH(s) \xrightarrow{H_2O} Na^+(aq) + OH^-(aq)$	–44.51
$NH_4Cl(s) \xrightarrow{H_2O} NH_4^+(aq) + Cl^-(aq)$	+14.78
$NH_4NO_3(s) \xrightarrow{H_2O} NH_4^+(aq) + NO_3^-(aq)$	+25.69
$NaCl(s) \xrightarrow{H_2O} Na^+(aq) + Cl^-(aq)$	+3.88
$LiBr(s) \xrightarrow{H_2O} Li^+(aq) + Br^-(aq)$	–48.83
$H^+(aq) + OH^-(aq) \longrightarrow H_2O(\ell)$	–55.8

*The ΔH values are based on molar quantities represented in the equations. A minus sign indicates an exothermic reaction.

Table I

Reading the Table:

♦ Notice the title of this table: *Heats of Reaction at 101.3 kPa and 298 K.* This is simply telling you that all reactions discussed here are taking place at 298 K and at standard pressure 101.3 kPa. Many questions on the table will include this detail, but keep in mind that it is not an integral part of the question.

♦ The table is split into three different kinds of chemical reactions:

➔ **Top:** *combustion* reactions – chemical reactions in which organic compounds (see **Tables P, Q & R**) combine with oxygen and produce carbon dioxide, water and energy in the form of heat and light (AKA burning)

⇨ Ex: $CH_4(g) + 2O_2(g) \longrightarrow CO_2(g) + 2H_2O(\ell)$ CH_4 and O_2 combine, forming CO_2 and water (the energy produced is not shown in the reaction)

➔ **Middle:** *synthesis* reactions – result in compounds *"formed from their elements."*

⇨ Ex: $C(s) + O_2(g) \longrightarrow CO_2(g)$ C and O_2 combine, forming CO_2 (8th from top)

⇨ Ex: $2C(s) + H_2(g) \longrightarrow C_2H_2(g)$ C and H_2 combine, forming C_2H_2 (9th from bottom)

➔ **Bottom:** compounds *dissolving in water* by separating into the different ions that the substance is formed from (An $\xrightarrow{H_2O}$ arrow with H_2O on top indicates dissolving)

⇨ Ex: $NaCl(s) \xrightarrow{H_2O} Na^+(aq) + Cl^-(aq)$ NaCl separates into Na^+ and Cl^-

♦ To the right of each chemical reaction, the ΔH value is indicated. (See gray box above.) The **asterisk (*)** on top of the column corresponds to a note underneath the table, which tells you

two important pieces of information:

> *The ΔH values are based on molar quantities represented in the equations. A minus sign indicates an exothermic reaction.

➔ *"The ΔH values are based on molar quantities represented in the equations."* This means that if the ΔH value for a specific equation is, say, +66.4 kJ, this amount of heat is only accurate for the specific molar amounts, meaning the *coefficients*, written in this reaction. If the coefficients (molar amounts) were doubled or halved, so would the amount of energy absorbed or released be doubled or halved as well.

⇨ Ex: See the reaction 10th from the top: $N_2(g) + O_2(g) \rightarrow 2NO(g)$. This equation has a ΔH of **+182.6 kJ**. This number is only accurate when discussing a reaction producing the same amount of *NO(g)* as in this reaction: **2 mol.** (See the coefficient in front of *NO(g)*.)

      ✓ If asked how much heat is absorbed when producing **1 mol** of *NO(g)* from its elements, *halve* the value stated on the table: **90.3 kJ**.

      ✓ If asked how much heat is absorbed when producing **4 mol** of *NO(g)* from its elements, *double* the value stated on the table: **365.2 kJ**.

➔ *"A minus sign indicates an exothermic reaction."* Notice that some values in the ΔH column have a *minus (-)* sign before and others have a *plus (+)* sign. This is one way to differentiate between **endothermic** and **exothermic** reactions. The values with a **plus** sign represent **_endothermic_** reactions, while those with a **minus** sign represent **_exothermic_** reactions. (No need to memorize – this information is right there!)

⇨   When asked in a multiple-choice question which reaction *releases* the most heat, begin by looking up the ΔH values of each given reaction. Eliminate the choices with values with plus signs. These represent endothermic reactions, which absorb, rather than release, heat.

⇨   The same is true regarding the opposite – when asked which reaction *absorbs* the most heat, you'd eliminate the reactions with a negative ΔH and focus on those with the plus signs.

⇨   **Note:** The *minus* sign is NOT representing a negative amount of heat released. The amount of heat gained or released in any reaction is **always positive**. The plus/minus signs simply indicate whether the reaction is **endo**thermic or **exo**thermic. The *number* represents the amount of energy that is being absorbed or released.

      ✓ If asked for the value of ΔH for a specific reaction, *include the minus or plus sign* in your answer.

      ✓ But if asked *how much heat is absorbed or released*, **don't** include the *sign*. Just give the number.

Table I

Examples:

1. Which of the following 4 chemical reactions releases the most heat?

✓	$N_2(g) + 3H_2(g) \longrightarrow 2NH_3(g)$
✓	$2C(s) + 3H_2(g) \longrightarrow C_2H_6(g)$
✓	$2C(s) + 2H_2(g) \longrightarrow C_2H_4(g)$
✓	$2C(s) + H_2(g) \longrightarrow C_2H_2(g)$

➜ To answer this question, your first step is determining which of these reactions involve the release of heat, or in other words, which reactions are exothermic. Use the ΔH values on the table to help you figure this out. Notice that the first 2 choices have negative ΔH values, and the next 2 choices have positive ΔH values.

➜ Eliminate choices 3 and 4, because since they are endothermic reactions, they absorb heat rather than release heat.

➜ Choose between choices 1 & 2. **Choice 1** is the correct answer, since 91.8 is greater than 84.0. (Again – these are not negative numbers. The minus sign just indicates that reaction is exothermic. If the numbers would be negative, -84.0 would be greater.)

2. What is the net (total) amount of heat absorbed when four moles of HI are formed from its elements at 101.3 kPa and 298 K?

➜ To answer this question, first find the reaction this question is discussing. Since HI is being formed "from its elements," you're looking for a reaction with HI as the product (right side) and H and I as the reactants (left side). This reaction is the eighth one from the bottom. It looks like this: $H_2(g) + I_2(g) \longrightarrow 2HI(g)$

➜ Next, to find the amount of heat absorbed in this reaction, look at the ΔH value to the right of the reaction. It is +53.0. The plus sign indicates an endothermic reaction, and the number tells you how much heat is absorbed. **But this is <u>not</u> your answer!**

➜ Remember: *"The ΔH values are based on molar quantities represented in the equations."* Look at the coefficient in front of HI. It is a 2. That means that for every *two* moles of HI produced in this reaction, 53 kJ of heat are absorbed. Since the question is asking how much heat is absorbed when *four* moles are produced, double the amount of heat provided. Your answer is **106.0 kJ.**

3. Based on Table I, which compound dissolves in water by an exothermic process?

- ✓ LiBr
- ✓ NH_4NO_3
- ✓ KNO_3

➜ First locate these compounds. Since they are dissolving in water, they must be on the bottom section of the table. They are second, fourth and seventh from the bottom.

➜ Then, based on the plus or minus sign to the right of the equations, determine which compound dissolves by an exothermic process. The correct answer is **choice 1.**

1. Based on Table I, which compound dissolves in water by an exothermic process?
   - (1) NaCl
   - (2) NaOH
   - (3) NH_4Cl
   - (4) NH_4NO_3

2. Based on Table I, what is the ΔH value for the production of 1.00 mole of $NO_2(g)$ from its elements at 101.3 kPa and 298 K?
   - (1) +33.2 kJ
   - (2) -33.2 kJ
   - (3) +132.8 kJ
   - (4) -132.8 kJ

3. What is the net amount of heat released when two moles of $C_2H_6(g)$ are formed from its elements at 101.3 kPa and 298 K?
   - (1) 42.0 kJ
   - (2) 84.0 kJ
   - (3) 126.0 kJ
   - (4) 168.0 kJ

4. According to Table I, which equation represents a change resulting in the greatest quantity of energy released?
   - (1) $2C(s) + 3H_2(g) \rightarrow C_2H_6(g)$
   - (2) $2C(s) + 2H_2(g) \rightarrow C_2H_4(g)$
   - (3) $N_2(g) + 3H_2(g) \rightarrow 2NH_3(g)$
   - (4) $N_2(g) + O_2(g) \rightarrow 2NO(g)$

5. At 101.3 kPa and 298 K, what is the total amount of heat released when one mole of aluminum oxide, $Al_2O_3(s)$, is formed from its elements?
   - (1) 393.5 kJ
   - (2) 837.8 kJ
   - (3) 1676 kJ
   - (4) 3351 kJ

6. Which compound is formed from its elements by an exothermic reaction at 298 K and 101.3 kPa?
   - (1) $C_2H_4(g)$
   - (2) HI(g)
   - (3) $H_2O(g)$
   - (4) $NO_2(g)$

7. At 101.3 kPa and 298 K, a 1.0-mole sample of which compound absorbs the greatest amount of heat as the entire sample dissolves in water?
   - (1) LiBr
   - (2) NaCl
   - (3) NaOH
   - (4) NH_4Cl

8. *Given the balanced equation representing a reaction at 101.3 kPa and 298 K:*

   $N_2(g) + 3H_2(g) \rightarrow 2NH_3(g) + 91.8$ kJ

   Which statement is true about this reaction?
   - (1) It is exothermic and ΔH is −91.8 kJ.
   - (2) It is exothermic and ΔH is +91.8 kJ.
   - (3) It is endothermic and ΔH is −91.8 kJ.
   - (4) It is endothermic and ΔH is +91.8 kJ.

9. *Given the reaction at 101.3 kilopascals and 298 K:*

   hydrogen gas + iodine gas → hydrogen iodide gas

   This reaction is classified as
   - (1) endothermic, because heat is absorbed
   - (2) endothermic, because heat is released
   - (3) exothermic, because heat is absorbed
   - (4) exothermic, because heat is released

NEW YORK STATE
CHEMISTRY REFERENCE TABLES

TABLE J

ACTIVITY SERIES

Table J Activity Series**			
Most Active	Metals	Nonmetals	Most Active
	Li	F₂	
	Rb	Cl₂	
	K	Br₂	
	Cs	I₂	
	Ba		
	Sr		
	Ca		
	Na		
	Mg		
	Al		
	Ti		
	Mn		
	Zn		
	Cr		
	Fe		
	Co		
	Ni		
	Sn		
	Pb		
	H₂		
	Cu		
	Ag		
Least Active	Au		Least Active

**Activity Series is based on the hydrogen standard. H₂ is *not* a metal.

TABLE J: Activity Series

Table J lists common *metals* and *nonmetals* and shows their ***relative activity levels***.

The more **active** an element is, the *more likely it is to react* in a chemical equation and vice versa.

→ Active **metals** *oxidize* (*lose* electrons in redox reactions) more easily.

→ Active **nonmetals** are *reduced* (*gain* electrons in redox reactions) more easily.

Reading the Table:

♦ The table is split into two parts: **METALS** and **NONMETALS**.

→ **Note:** As indicated by the double asterisk (**) on top of the table and the corresponding note on the bottom, H_2 **(hydrogen) is** *not* **a metal**, although it is found listed among the metals. It is simply put there for reference purposes. (See below.)

♦ As shown on the right and left sides of the table, the elements are listed according to *how active/reactive they are*. The most active elements are higher up, and the less active elements are lower down.

Table J Activity Series**

Most Active	Metals	Nonmetals	Most Active
	Li	F_2	
	Rb	Cl_2	
	K	Br_2	
	Cs	I_2	
	Ba		
	Sr		
	Ca		
	Na		
	Mg		
	Al		
	Ti		
	Mn		
	Zn		
	Cr		
	Fe		
	Co		
	Ni		
	Sn		
	Pb		
	H_2		
	Cu		
	Ag		
Least Active	Au		Least Active

**Activity Series is based on the hydrogen standard. H_2 is *not* a metal.

♦ Using the above information and <u>the following guidelines</u>, you can answer most regents questions on this table:

➔ <u>Rule 1:</u> In a **single replacement reaction**, a metal will react *spontaneously* (on its own) with a **compound** (by replacing the metal in the compound) if it is **more active** than the metal part of the compound. Activity levels are determined by using Table J. A **nonmetal** will react spontaneously with a compound if it is more active than the **nonmetal** part of the compound. (Metals will replace metals and nonmetals will replace nonmetals.)

⇨ Will **Ca** react spontaneously with **ZnO**?

✓ <u>Check:</u> Is Ca more active than the metal part of the compound - Zn?

✓ Ca is *above* Zn on Table J. Therefore, it must be more active than Zn – so it *will* react spontaneously with ZnO, forming CaO and giving off Zn metal.

⇨ Will **Br** react spontaneously with **NaCl**?

✓ Br is a nonmetal (see **NONMETAL** column) but is *below* Cl, the nonmetal in the formula NaCl. Br is therefore less active than Cl and will *not* react spontaneously with NaCl.

➔ <u>Rule 2:</u> *A metal that is more active than H_2 (above it on Table J) will react spontaneously with an* **acid** *to produce* **hydrogen gas**. Notice that only 3 metals are below H_2. (Most acids begin with an H. The most common acid given is HCl.)

⇨ Will **Fe** react with **HCl(aq)** to produce hydrogen gas?

✓ Since Fe is *above* H_2 on Table J, it *will* react with HCl.

➔ <u>Rule 3:</u> The more *active* a metal is, the more easily it is *oxidized*. In an electrochemical cell, the metal that is on top on Table J will be oxidized (**anode**), while the metal underneath will be reduced (**cathode**).

⇨ Identify one metal from Table J that is more easily oxidized than **K**.

✓ More easily oxidized = more active. Possible answers: **Rb, Li**

1. Which metal reacts spontaneously with $NiCl_2(aq)$?
   (1) Au(s)   (2) Cu(s) (3) Sn(s) (4) Zn(s)

2. Which metal reacts spontaneously with Sr^{2+} ions?
   (1) Ca(s)   (2) Co(s) (3) Cs(s) (4) Cu(s)

3. Which reaction occurs spontaneously?
   (1) $Cl_2(g) + 2NaBr(aq) \rightarrow Br_2(\ell) + 2NaCl(aq)$
   (2) $Cl_2(g) + 2NaF(aq) \rightarrow F_2(g) + 2NaCl(aq)$
   (3) $I_{2((}s) + 2NaBr(aq) \rightarrow Br_2(\ell) + 2NaI(aq)$
   (4) $I_2(s) + 2NaF(aq) \rightarrow F_2(g) + 2NaI(aq)$

4. Which element reacts spontaneously with 1.0 M HCl(aq) at room temperature?
   (1) Copper   (2) gold (3) silver (4) zinc

5. Which metal will spontaneously react with $Zn^{2+}(aq)$, but will not spontaneously react with $Mg^{2+}(aq)$?
   (1) Mn(s) (2) Cu(s)   (3) Ni(s) (4) Ba(s)

6. A student sets up a voltaic cell using magnesium and zinc electrodes. The ionic equation below represents this operating cell.
   $Mg(s) + Zn^{2+} + (aq) \rightarrow Zn(s) + Mg^{2+} + (aq)$

   State, in terms of the relative activity of metals, why the reaction in this cell occurs.

7. Identify one metal from Reference Table J that is more easily oxidized than Mg(s).

8. *A student develops the list shown below that includes laboratory equipment and materials for constructing a voltaic cell.*
   Laboratory Equipment and Materials
   - a strip of zinc
   - a strip of copper

   Compare the activities of the two metals used by the student for constructing the voltaic cell. *(State which metal is more/less active than the other.)*

9. *In a laboratory investigation, magnesium reacts with hydrochloric acid to produce hydrogen gas and magnesium chloride. This reaction is represented by the unbalanced equation below.*
   $Mg(s) + HCl(aq)$
   $\rightarrow H_2(g) + MgCl_2(aq)$
   State, in terms of the relative activity of elements, why this reaction is spontaneous.

10. Based on Reference Table J, identify one metal that does not react spontaneously with HCl(aq).

11. *Because tap water is slightly acidic, water pipes made of iron corrode over time, as shown by the balanced ionic equation below:*
    $2Fe + 6H^+ + \rightarrow 2Fe^{3+} + + 3H_2$
    Explain, in terms of chemical reactivity, why copper pipes are less likely to corrode than iron pipes.

12. Explain, in terms of activity, why HCl(aq) reacts with Zn(s), but HCl(aq) does not react with Cu(s).

NEW YORK STATE
CHEMISTRY REFERENCE TABLES

TABLES K, L, M

COMMON ACIDS
COMMON BASES
COMMON ACID-BASE INDICATORS

Table K
Common Acids

Formula	Name
HCl(aq)	hydrochloric acid
HNO$_2$(aq)	nitrous acid
HNO$_3$(aq)	nitric acid
H$_2$SO$_3$(aq)	sulfurous acid
H$_2$SO$_4$(aq)	sulfuric acid
H$_3$PO$_4$(aq)	phosphoric acid
H$_2$CO$_3$(aq) or CO$_2$(aq)	carbonic acid
CH$_3$COOH(aq) or HC$_2$H$_3$O$_2$(aq)	ethanoic acid (acetic acid)

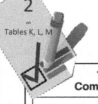

2
or
Tables K, L, M

Table L
Common Bases

Formula	Name
NaOH(aq)	sodium hydroxide
KOH(aq)	potassium hydroxide
Ca(OH)$_2$(aq)	calcium hydroxide
NH$_3$(aq)	aqueous ammonia

Table M
Common Acid–Base Indicators

Indicator	Approximate pH Range for Color Change	Color Change
methyl orange	3.1–4.4	red to yellow
bromthymol blue	6.0–7.6	yellow to blue
phenolphthalein	8–9	colorless to pink
litmus	4.5–8.3	red to blue
bromcresol green	3.8–5.4	yellow to blue
thymol blue	8.0–9.6	yellow to blue

Source: *The Merck Index*, 14th ed., 2006, Merck Publishing Group

TABLES K & L: Common Acids & Common Bases

Table K
Common Acids

Formula	Name
HCl(aq)	hydrochloric acid
HNO_2(aq)	nitrous acid
HNO_3(aq)	nitric acid
H_2SO_3(aq)	sulfurous acid
H_2SO_4(aq)	sulfuric acid
H_3PO_4(aq)	phosphoric acid
H_2CO_3(aq) or CO_2(aq)	carbonic acid
CH_3COOH(aq) or $HC_2H_3O_2$(aq)	ethanoic acid (acetic acid)

Table L
Common Bases

Formula	Name
NaOH(aq)	sodium hydroxide
KOH(aq)	potassium hydroxide
$Ca(OH)_2$(aq)	calcium hydroxide
NH_3(aq)	aqueous ammonia

Reading the Tables:

♦ Each table has a **FORMULA** column where it lists the acid or base's *chemical formula* in *symbols* and a **NAME** column where it gives the acid or base's *IUPAC (official scientific) name*.

♦ Notice that all formulas end with **(aq)**, which stands for "aqueous." This means that the compound is dissolved in water. All acids and bases are aqueous.

Tables **K & L** list the formulas and names of common **Arrhenius acids** and **bases**. Use these tables to help determine whether a compound is an acid or a base or to match a compound's name to its formula and vice versa.

Arrhenius acids → yield **H⁺** (hydronium) ions in aqueous solutions. Their formula often begins with **H**.

Arrhenius bases → yield **OH⁻** (hydroxide) ions in aqueous solutions. Their formula often ends in **OH**.

In other words, according to Arrhenius, an acid is a substance that, when dissolved in water, produces **H⁺ ions** (hydrogen atoms with a positive charge) as the **only positive ions** in the solution. There will be other ions in the solution, but those will be *negative*.

Similarly, Arrhenius defines a base as a substance that, when dissolved in water, produces **OH⁻** (hydroxide) **ions** as the **only negative ions** in the solution. There will be other ions, but those will be *positive*.

More Information on Acids & Bases:

Acids and bases…

→ Are *electrolytes* – compounds that conduct electricity when dissolved in water (**Salts** – ionic compounds – are also electrolytes)

→ Cause indicators to change color (as discussed further under **TABLE M: Common Acid-Base Indicators**)

→ Neutralize each other when combined, forming water and a salt (ionic compound)

Acids…

→ React with most metals to release bubbles of hydrogen gas (see **Table J**)

♦ This table is most often used for identifying compounds as Arrhenius acids or bases (see gray box above). When given a list of compounds and asked to identify the Arrhenius acid or base, the easiest way to do so is find one of the choices on either of the two tables.

♦ <u>Helpful hints:</u>

➔ Most acids on Table K (Arrhenius acids) have formulas that begin with hydrogen, H. The last two acids on the table, *carbonic acid* and *ethanoic acid*, each have two possible ways to represent their chemical formulas – one beginning with H and one not.

➔ All bases on Table L *but NH₃* end in OH, **hydroxide**.

➔ <u>Note:</u> It is easy to mistakenly identify ethanoic acid (CH_3COOH) as a base, since its formula ends in OH. However, here's a rule to keep in mind: **Bases *never* contain <u>carbon (C)</u> within their formulas**.

♦ To identify an ***electrolyte*** (a compound that conducts electricity when dissolved in water) among a few choices, look for an *acid*, *base* or a *salt* (ionic compound), since they are all electrolytes.

----

1. Which substance is an Arrhenius base?
   (1) HNO_3 (3) $Ca(OH)_2$
   (2) H_2SO_3 (4) CH_3COOH

2. Which compound when dissolved in water is an Arrhenius acid?
   (1) CH_3OH (3) $NaCl$
   (2) CH_3COOCH_3 (4) H_3PO_4

3. Which substance is an electrolyte?
   (1) CCl_4 (3) SiO_2
   (2) $C_6H_{12}O_6$ (4) H_2SO_4

4. What is the chemical name for $H_2SO_3(aq)$?
   (1) sulfuric acid   (3) hydrosulfuric acid
   (2) sulfurous acid   (4) hydrosulfurous acid

5. Which compound is an electrolyte?
   (1) H_2O (3) CO_2
   (2) C_2H_6 (4) CH_3OH

TABLE M: Common Acid-Base Indicators

Table M
Common Acid–Base Indicators

Indicator	Approximate pH Range for Color Change	Color Change
methyl orange	3.1–4.4	red to yellow
bromthymol blue	6.0–7.6	yellow to blue
phenolphthalein	8–9	colorless to pink
litmus	4.5–8.3	red to blue
bromcresol green	3.8–5.4	yellow to blue
thymol blue	8.0–9.6	yellow to blue

Source: *The Merck Index*, 14th ed., 2006, Merck Publishing Group

Reading the Table:

♦ The **COLOR CHANGE** column (right) tells you what colors the **INDICATOR** (left) will be, depending on the **pH of the solution:**

➜ The *first* color mentioned is the color of the solution if the pH of the solution is *below* the **pH range for color change** (middle column).

➜ The *second* color mentioned is the color of the solution if the solution's pH is *above* the pH range for color change.

➜ If the solution has a pH *within* the pH range for color change it will be a *third* color – the combination of the two colors mentioned (i.e. orange if red to yellow or green if yellow to blue etc.).

Table M lists *common acid-base indicators*, their *pH ranges for color changes* and the *colors* each indicator will be above and below this pH range.

Indicator → a liquid that changes color when added to acids or bases, depending on the strength of the acid or base. Each indicator listed has a specific **pH range** within which it will change its color.

pH scale → a scale that measures the strengths of acids and bases.

➜ The pH scale ranges from 1 to **14**, 1 being the strongest acid and 14 being the strongest base. Substances with a pH of **7** are **neutral** – neither acidic nor basic.

➜ The pH scale measures the **concentration of hydronium (hydrogen) ions** within the solution. Substances with higher concentrations of hydronium ions are more acidic, and substances with lower concentrations of hydronium ions are more basic.

➜ Each number on the pH scale represents changes by **factors of ten**. Each *lower* number on the pH scale represents a tenfold *increase* in hydronium ion concentration in the solution. Each *higher* number on the pH scale represents a tenfold *decrease* in hydronium ion concentration in the solution.

⇨ A solution with a pH of **3** is *10 times more acidic* than a solution with a pH of **4**.

⇨ A solution with a pH of **2** is *100 times more acidic* than a solution with a pH of **4** (10 X 10)

⇨ <u>Ex1</u>: **Methyl orange**'s pH range for color change is **3.1-4.4**, and it changes from **red to yellow**.

  ✓ This means that if methyl orange is put into a solution with a pH *below 3.1*, it will be **red**.

  ✓ If it is put into a solution with a pH *above 4.4*, it will be **yellow**.

  ✓ If it is put into a solution with a pH *between 3.1 and 4.4*, it will be **orange**.

⇨ <u>Ex2:</u> **Phenolphthalein**'s pH range for color change is **8-9**, and it changes from **colorless to pink**.

  ✓ This means that if phenolphthalein is put into a solution with a pH *below 8*, it will become **colorless**.

  ✓ If it is put into a solution with a pH *above 9*, it will turn **pink**.

  ✓ If the solution has a pH *between 8 and 9*, the phenolphthalein will be **between colorless and pink** (a very light shade of pink).

♦ <u>Note:</u> Only three of the six indicators on the table can *completely differentiate* between acids and bases – **bromthymol blue, litmus** and **phenolphthalein**. The other three indicators can indicate the *strength* of an acidic or basic solution, but they can't always differentiate between the two. (Phenolphthalein is used to differentiate between acid and base in the titration experiment. When the solution is an acid or neutral, it will be colorless – see through. When the solution is a base, the solution is not colorless – it is either a light pink or a darker pink, depending on the strength of the base.)

  ➔ When a solution with **thymol blue** added to it turns *yellow*, this only indicates that *its pH is less than 8*. It may be an acid (if its pH is less than 7), and it may be a base (if its pH is more than 7.) However, if this solution turns blue, it must be basic (because its pH is above 9.6).

  ➔ On the contrary, when a solution with **litmus** added to it turns *red*, it is certain that the solution is *acidic* (with a pH below 4.5). If it turns *blue*, the solution must be **basic** (with a pH above 8.3). Only if the litmus turns *purple* (mix of red and blue) is it still uncertain – because this means the pH of this solution is between 4.5 and 8.3 → it may be acidic, and it may be basic.

1. The table to the right shows the molar concentrations of hydronium ion, H_3O^+, in four different solutions.

   Molar Concentration of H_3O^+ Ions in Four Solutions

Solution	Molar Concentration of H_3O^+ Ion (M)
A	0.1
B	0.01
C	0.001
D	0.0001

   Which solution has the highest pH?
   (1) A   (2) B   (3) C   (4) D

2. Which statement describes characteristics of a 0.01 M KOH(aq) solution?
   (1) The solution is acidic with a pH less than 7.
   (2) The solution is acidic with a pH greater than 7.
   (3) The solution is basic with a pH less than 7.
   (4) The solution is basic with a pH greater than 7.

3. *When the concentration of hydrogen ions in a solution is decreased by a factor of ten, the pH of the solution
   (1) increases by 1   (3) decreases by 1
   (2) increases by 10 (4) decreases by 10

4. How are HNO_3(aq) and CH_3COOH(aq) similar?
   (1) They are Arrhenius acids and they turn blue litmus red.
   (2) They are Arrhenius acids and they turn red litmus blue.
   (3) They are Arrhenius bases and they turn blue litmus red.
   (4) They are Arrhenius bases and they turn red litmus blue.

5. *Compared to a 1.0-liter aqueous solution with a pH of 7.0, a 1.0-liter aqueous solution with a pH of 5.0 contains
   (1) 10 times more hydronium ions
   (2) 100 times more hydronium ions
   (3) 10 times more hydroxide ions
   (4) 100 times more hydroxide ions

Questions 6-9: *In a laboratory investigation, an HCl(aq) solution with a pH value of 2 is used to determine the molarity of a KOH(aq) solution. A 7.5-milliliter sample of the KOH(aq) is exactly neutralized by 15.0 milliliters of the 0.010 M HCl(aq). During this laboratory activity, appropriate safety equipment is used, and safety procedures are followed.*

6. *Determine the pH value of a solution that is ten times less acidic than the HCl(aq) solution.

7. State the color of the indicator bromcresol green if it is added to a sample of the KOH(aq) solution.

8. State the color of methyl orange indicator after the indicator is placed in a solution of 0.10 M NH_3(aq).

9. Identify two indicators from Reference Table M that are yellow in solutions with a pH of 5.5.

Questions 10-11: *Some carbonated beverages are made by forcing carbon dioxide gas into a beverage solution. When a bottle of one kind of carbonated beverage is first opened, the beverage has a pH value of 3.*

10. State, in terms of the pH scale, why this beverage is classified as acidic.

11. Using Table M, identify one indicator that is yellow in a solution with the same pH value as this beverage.

Questions 12-13: *A student is to perform a laboratory test to determine the pH value of two different solutions. The student is given one bottle containing a solution with a pH of 2.0 and another bottle containing a solution with a pH of 5.0. The student is also given six dropping bottles, each containing a different indicator listed in Reference Table M.*

12. Identify an indicator in Reference Table M that would differentiate the two solutions.

13. Compare the hydronium ion concentration of the solution having a pH of 2.0 to the hydronium ion concentration of the other solution given to the student.

Questions 14-16: *A student used blue litmus paper and phenolphthalein paper as indicators to test the pH of distilled water and five aqueous household solutions. Then the student used a pH meter to measure the pH of the distilled water and each solution. The results of the student's work are recorded in the table below.*

Testing Results

Liquid Tested	Color of Blue Litmus Paper	Color of Phenolphthalein Paper	Measured pH Value Using a pH Meter
2% milk	blue	colorless	6.4
distilled water	blue	colorless	7.0
household ammonia	blue	pink	11.5
lemon juice	red	colorless	2.3
tomato juice	red	colorless	4.3
vinegar	red	colorless	3.3

14. Identify the liquid tested that has the lowest hydronium ion concentration.

15. Explain, in terms of the pH range for color change on Reference Table M, why litmus is not appropriate to differentiate the acidity levels of tomato juice and vinegar.

16. Based on the measured pH values, identify the liquid tested that is 10 times more acidic than vinegar.

My Notes on the Previous Section(s):

_____

_____

_____

_____

_____

_____

_____

_____

_____

_____

_____

_____

_____

_____

_____

_____

_____

_____

_____

_____

_____

_____

_____

_____

_____

_____

_____

NEW YORK STATE
CHEMISTRY REFERENCE TABLES

TABLES N & O

SELECTED RADIOISOTOPES
SYMBOLS USED IN NUCLEAR CHEMISTRY

3
on
Tables N, O

Table N
Selected Radioisotopes

Nuclide	Half-Life	Decay Mode	Nuclide Name
^{198}Au	2.695 d	β^-	gold-198
^{14}C	5715 y	β^-	carbon-14
^{37}Ca	182 ms	β^+	calcium-37
^{60}Co	5.271 y	β^-	cobalt-60
^{137}Cs	30.2 y	β^-	cesium-137
^{53}Fe	8.51 min	β^+	iron-53
^{220}Fr	27.4 s	α	francium-220
^{3}H	12.31 y	β^-	hydrogen-3
^{131}I	8.021 d	β^-	iodine-131
^{37}K	1.23 s	β^+	potassium-37
^{42}K	12.36 h	β^-	potassium-42
^{85}Kr	10.73 y	β^-	krypton-85
^{16}N	7.13 s	β^-	nitrogen-16
^{19}Ne	17.22 s	β^+	neon-19
^{32}P	14.28 d	β^-	phosphorus-32
^{239}Pu	2.410×10^4 y	α	plutonium-239
^{226}Ra	1599 y	α	radium-226
^{222}Rn	3.823 d	α	radon-222
^{90}Sr	29.1 y	β^-	strontium-90
^{99}Tc	2.13×10^5 y	β^-	technetium-99
^{232}Th	1.40×10^{10} y	α	thorium-232
^{233}U	1.592×10^5 y	α	uranium-233
^{235}U	7.04×10^8 y	α	uranium-235
^{238}U	4.47×10^9 y	α	uranium-238

Source: CRC Handbook of Chemistry and Physics, 91st ed., 2010–2011, CRC Press

Table O
Symbols Used in Nuclear Chemistry

Name	Notation	Symbol
alpha particle	$^{4}_{2}He$ or $^{4}_{2}\alpha$	α
beta particle	$^{0}_{-1}e$ or $^{0}_{-1}\beta$	β^-
gamma radiation	$^{0}_{0}\gamma$	γ
neutron	$^{1}_{0}n$	n
proton	$^{1}_{1}H$ or $^{1}_{1}p$	p
positron	$^{0}_{+1}e$ or $^{0}_{+1}\beta$	β^+

TABLE N: Selected Radioisotopes

Table N
Selected Radioisotopes

Nuclide	Half-Life	Decay Mode	Nuclide Name
^{198}Au	2.695 d	β^-	gold-198
^{14}C	5715 y	β^-	carbon-14
^{37}Ca	182 ms	β^+	calcium-37
^{60}Co	5.271 y	β^-	cobalt-60
^{137}Cs	30.2 y	β^-	cesium-137
^{53}Fe	8.51 min	β^+	iron-53
^{220}Fr	27.4 s	α	francium-220
^{3}H	12.31 y	β^-	hydrogen-3
^{131}I	8.021 d	β^-	iodine-131
^{37}K	1.23 s	β^+	potassium-37
^{42}K	12.36 h	β^-	potassium-42
^{85}Kr	10.73 y	β^-	krypton-85
^{16}N	7.13 s	β^-	nitrogen-16
^{19}Ne	17.22 s	β^+	neon-19
^{32}P	14.28 d	β^-	phosphorus-32
^{239}Pu	2.410×10^4 y	α	plutonium-239
^{226}Ra	1599 y	α	radium-226
^{222}Rn	3.823 d	α	radon-222
^{90}Sr	29.1 y	β^-	strontium-90
^{99}Tc	2.13×10^5 y	β^-	technetium-99
^{232}Th	1.40×10^{10} y	α	thorium-232
^{233}U	1.592×10^5 y	α	uranium-233
^{235}U	7.04×10^8 y	α	uranium-235
^{238}U	4.47×10^9 y	α	uranium-238

Source: CRC Handbook of Chemistry and Physics, 91st ed., 2010–2011, CRC Press

Reading the Table:

♦ The **NUCLIDE** and **NUCLIDE NAME** columns go together:

➔ The **NUCLIDE** column, furthest to the left, lists selected radioisotopes in shorthand, in alphabetical order.

⇨ The letters on the bottom represent the element's **symbol**, and the small # on top represents the **total mass** of the atom. (It is called a nuclide since the number represents the mass of the atom's nucleus, the location of the protons and neutrons.)

Tables **N** lists *selected radioisotopes* along with their **nuclides** (shorthand symbol), **half-lives**, **decay modes** and **nuclide names**.

Isotopes → atoms of the same element with *different numbers* of **neutrons** and therefore *different mass numbers* (mass number → sum of protons and neutrons)

Radioisotope → **radioactive isotope** → an unstable isotope ("version") of an element that spontaneously emits (lets out) *rays and particles* (different forms of radiation) from its nucleus in order to become stable. (They turn into different, stable elements via this process.)

The specific kinds of rays or particles that each kind of radioactive element emits is its **decay mode**.

➔ All elements with an atomic number **above 83** are *unstable*. Elements with atomic numbers below 84 are usually stable, but some may have unstable isotopes.

➔ <u>Ex:</u> Carbon-12 (carbon with a mass of 12) is the more common isotope of carbon and is stable, yet **carbon-14** (carbon with a mass of 14) is unstable and will emit radiation to become stable.

Half-life → the amount of time it takes for half the mass of an unstable element (radioisotope) to decay. Every element has a unique half-life, which **always remains constant** despite changes in *pressure*, *temperature* or *mass*.

➔ <u>Ex:</u> Calcium-37 has a half-life of 182 ms. That means that every 182 milliseconds, the mass of a block of ^{37}Ca will split in half. Half of it will decay into another element and half will remain ^{37}Ca.

➔ The **NUCLIDE NAME** column, furthest to the right, gives you the same information as the nuclide column, but includes the name of the radioactive element instead of its symbol.

> ✓ Ex: ^{198}Au stands for **gold-198**, or gold with a mass of 198.

> ⇨ To figure out how many protons a specific nuclide has, either use its *symbol* on the PT or its *name* on Table S to look up its atomic number. Au-198 has **97** protons.

> ⇨ To figure out how many *neutrons* a nuclide has, **subtract** the number of protons (its atomic number) from the total mass (given for the specific isotope) of the atom. Au-198 has **101** neutrons (198-97=101)

♦ The **HALF-LIFE** column tells you each radioisotope's *half-life*, which can range from a few milliseconds (ms) to thousands of years (y).

> ➔ Table D: Selected Units tells you which unit of time each symbol (s, min, d...) in this column stands for.

Table D Selected Units		
Symbol	Name	Quantity
s	second	time
min	minute	time
h	hour	time
d	day	time
y	year	time

> ➔ As explained in the box above, a half-life is *the amount of time it takes for half of a radioisotope's mass to decay* into a new element or an isotope of the same element.

> > ⇨ Ex: ^{53}Fe/iron-53 has a half-life of **8.51 minutes**.

> > > ✓ This means that if a block of iron-53 started out with a mass of 50 grams, after one half-life, 8.51 minutes, it will now have a mass of 25 grams, or ½ of what it was previously. (The other 25 grams became a different element.)

> > > ✓ After a second half-life, another 8.51 minutes, the block will have a mass of 12.5 grams, ¼ of its original mass.

> > > ✓ After a third half-life, another 8.51 minutes, it will have a mass of 6.25 grams – $^1/_8$ of its original mass – and so on.

> > > ✓ Every 8.51 minutes, the mass of the block of iron-53 will become half of what it was previously.

> > ⇨ See below for a further discussion on solving half-life problems.

> ➔ The **DECAY MODE** column tells you, in symbols, which rays or particles the radioisotope will emit during its decay process.

> ➔ Use Table O: Symbols Used in Nuclear Chemistry to identify the symbols in this column.

⇨ Ex: **Carbon-14**'s decay mode is β^- and **Radon-222**'s decay mode is α. As you can see on Table O, these symbols stands for a **beta particle** and **alpha particle** respectively. (This table is discussed in more detail later on in this section.)

Solving Half-Life Problems:

◆ *How many grams of a 100-g sample of ^{198}Au remains unchanged after 16 days?* **To find the** *mass* **that remains:**

➔ Look up the radioisotope's half-life on Table N (if it isn't given to you).

⇨ Gold-198 has a half-life of **2.695 days**.

➔ Divide the amount of time that passed by the length of the half-life to figure out how many half-lives passed.

⇨ 16/2.695 ≅ **6 half-lives**

➔ Halve the original mass the amount of times as half-lives passed:

⇨ 100 ⤳ 50 ⤳ 25 ⤳ 12.5 ⤳ 6.25 ⤳ 3.125 ⤳ **1.5625 g**

◆ *What fraction of a 100-g sample of krypton-85 remains unchanged after 54 years?* **To find the** *fraction* **that remains:**

➔ Look up the radioisotope's half-life:

⇨ 10.73 years

➔ Divide time passed by length of half-life:

⇨ 54/10.73 ≅ 5 half-lives

➔ Divide 1 in half, then keep on dividing the resulting fraction in half the amount of times as half-lives passed:

⇨ 1 ⤳ ½ ⤳ ¼ ⤳ $^1/_8$ ⤳ $^1/_{16}$ ⤳ **$^1/_{32}$**

◆ *Determine the amount of time required for a 64.00-gram sample of strontonium-90 to decay until only 2.00 grams remains unchanged.* **To find the** *time* **until a specific mass remains:**

➔ Divide the original mass of the sample in half until you reach the desired mass. Count how many times you divided it (= how many half-lives passed).

⇨ 64 ⤳ 32 ⤳ 16 ⤳ 8 ⤳ 4 ⤳ **2**

⇨ 5 half-lives passed.

➔ Look up the radioisotope's half-life: **29.1 years**

➔ Multiply the number of half-lives that passed by the length of each half-life:

⇨ 5*29.1 = 145.5 years

♦ *Determine the total time that must elapse until only $^1/_8$ of an original sample of 16N remains unchanged.* **To find the *time* until a specific *fraction* remains:**

➔ Divide 1 in half, then keep on dividing the resulting fraction in half until you reach the desired fraction. Count how many times you divided 1 to get there (= how many half-lives passed):

⇨ $1 \xrightarrow{1} ½ \xrightarrow{2} ¼ \xrightarrow{3} {}^1/_8$

⇨ 3 half-lives passed.

➔ Look up the radioisotope's half-life: **7.13 seconds**

➔ Multiply the number of half-lives that passed by the length of each half-life:

⇨ 3*7.13 = 21.39 seconds

♦ *An original sample of I-129 has a mass of 60 grams. After 55 days, 1.625 grams of the original sample remains unchanged. What is the half-life of I-129?* **To find the *half-life* of a given radioisotope based on the *mass* that remains:**

➔ Halve the original mass until you get to the new mass. Count how many times you divided it (= how many half-lives passed).

⇨ $60 \xrightarrow{1} 30 \xrightarrow{2} 15 \xrightarrow{3} 7.5 \xrightarrow{4} 3.25 \xrightarrow{5}$ **1.625**

⇨ 5 half-lives passed.

➔ Divide the amount of time that passed by the number of half-lives to figure out the length of each half-life:

⇨ 55/5 = **11 days**

♦ *After decaying for 96 hours, $^1/_{16}$ of the original mass of a radioisotope sample remains unchanged. What is the half-life of this radioisotope?* **To find the *half-life* of a given radioisotope based on the *fraction* that remains:**

➔ Divide 1 in half, then keep on dividing the resulting fraction in half until you reach the fraction remaining. Count how many times you divided 1 to get there (= how many half-lives passed).

⇨ $1 \xrightarrow{1} ½ \xrightarrow{2} ¼ \xrightarrow{3} {}^1/_8 \xrightarrow{4} {}^1/_{16}$

⇨ 4 half-lives passed.

➔ Divide the amount of time that passed by the number of half-lives to figure out the length of each half-life:

⇨ 96/4 = 24 hours

TABLE O: Symbols Used in Nuclear Chemistry

Table O
Symbols Used in Nuclear Chemistry

Name	Notation	Symbol
alpha particle	^4_2He or $^4_2\alpha$	α
beta particle	$^0_{-1}e$ or $^0_{-1}\beta$	β^-
gamma radiation	$^0_0\gamma$	γ
neutron	^1_0n	n
proton	^1_1H or ^1_1p	p
positron	$^0_{+1}e$ or $^0_{+1}\beta$	β^+

Table O is used hand in hand with the **DECAY MODE** column on **Table N** and also on its own. It lists the *symbols* for the **subatomic particles and rays** emitted by decaying (radioactive) elements used in nuclear chemistry together with their *names* and shorthand *notations*.

Reading the Table:

♦ The **NAME** column tells you the name of the particle or radiation symbolized by the different Greek symbols in the **SYMBOL** column. Notice that only three of the symbols, the alpha particle, beta particle and positron, can be found on **Table N**. These are the most common particles naturally emitted by radioisotopes in their decay processes. Gamma rays are usually emitted along with other radiation.

♦ The **NOTATION** column shows you different **properties** of the subatomic particle or ray. This is the way they are represented in nuclear equations.

➔ The small number on **top** represents the mass of the particle. The small number on **bottom** represents the charge of the particle.

⇨ Ex: An **alpha particle** has a mass of **4** and a charge of **+2**. A **gamma ray** has a mass of **0** and a charge of **0** (no mass and no charge).

⇨ Notice that **beta particles** and **positrons** are quite similar – they only differ in their *charge*.

➔ The **letters** either represent a specific element or the symbol of the particle, as seen in the **SYMBOL** column.

⇨ The **alpha particle** can be represented as *He* or α, the alpha symbol. **Table S** tells you that *He* stands for the element **helium**. An alpha particle is the nucleus of a helium atom, which has a mass of 4 (2 protons plus 2 neutrons) and a charge of +2 (from the 2 protons).

⇨ A **beta particle** is represented by an *e* because it is an electron, which has a mass of 0 amu and a charge of -1. (Electrons, like all matter, *do* have mass, but since their mass is so insignificant compared to the mass of protons and neutrons, they are considered to have no mass.)

⇨ **Protons** are also represented by *H*, the symbol for **hydrogen**, since they are the same as the nucleus of a hydrogen atom, which has a mass of 1 and a charge of +1 (because it is composed of just 1 proton).

♦ Among the three first items on the chart, the **alpha particles** have the *least **penetrating power*** (are least strong) and **gamma rays** have the *most*, with **beta particles** coming somewhere *in between*.

Solving Nuclear Equations:

♦ *Transmutation* → the transformation of radioactive isotopes into new elements through their decay process. This process is modeled by **nuclear equations**.

➔ **Natural transmutation** → transmutation that happens *spontaneously*, on its own. There is only *one* reactant before the arrow.

⇨ <u>Ex:</u> In the following equation, **carbon** becomes **nitrogen** when it emits an electron: $^{14}_{6}C \rightarrow \,^{14}_{7}N + \,^{0}_{-1}e$

⇨ <u>Ex:</u> In the following equation, **calcium** becomes **potassium** when it emits an electron: $^{37}_{20}Ca \rightarrow \,^{37}_{19}K + \,^{0}_{-1}e$

➔ **Artificial transmutation** → an element's nucleus is *bombarded* with high energy particles, which causes it to emit radiation and change into a different element. There are *two* reactants – an element and a particle – before the arrow.

⇨ <u>Ex:</u> $^{235}_{92}Ca + \,^{1}_{0}n \rightarrow \,^{92}_{36}Kr + \,^{142}_{56}Ba + 2^{1}_{0}n + energy$

♦ <u>Solving Nuclear Equations:</u>

➔ The sum of the masses and charges on one side of the equation must equal the sum of the masses and charges on the other side of the equation.

⇨ Find the missing mass and charge by setting up individual equations for each one.

⇨ If the *element* is the unknown, identify it based on its charge/number of protons using the **PT** or **Table S**.

⇨ If the *particle* is the unknown, identify it using **Table O**.

→ <u>Example 1:</u> Complete the nuclear equation for the beta decay of Co-60 by writing an isotopic notation for the missing product: $^{60}_{27}Ca \rightarrow \, ^{0}_{-1}e + ^{?}_{?}?$

⇨ Find the missing mass:

✓ 60 = 0 + x; x = 60

✓ $^{60}_{?}?$

⇨ Find the missing charge:

✓ 27 = -1 + x; x = 28

✓ $^{60}_{28}?$

⇨ Look up atomic #28 (28 protons = a charge of 28) on the PT/Table S: $^{60}_{28}Ni$

→ <u>Example 2:</u> Complete the equation for the nuclear decay of Mo-99: $^{99}_{42}Mo \rightarrow \, ^{99}_{43}Tc + ^{?}_{?}?$

⇨ Find the missing mass:

✓ 99 = 99 + x; x = 0

✓ $^{0}_{?}?$

⇨ Find the missing charge:

✓ 42 = 43 + x; x = -1

✓ $^{0}_{-1}?$

⇨ Since it's the particle that's missing, use Table O to figure out which particle has a mass of 0 and charge of -1: $^{0}_{-1}e$ or $^{0}_{-1}\beta$ or β^-

→ <u>Example 3:</u> Complete the equation for the nuclear decay of I-108: $^{108}_{53}I \rightarrow \, ^{4}_{2}He + ^{?}_{?}?$

⇨ Find the missing mass:

✓ 108 = 4 + x; x = 104

✓ $^{104}_{?}?$

⇨ Find the missing charge:

✓ 53 = 2 + x

✓ $^{104}_{51}?$

⇨ Look up atomic #51 on the PT/Table S: $^{104}_{51}Sb$

1. A radioactive isotope has a half-life of 2.5 years. Which fraction of the original mass remains unchanged after 10. years?
   (1) 1/2   (3) 1/8
   (2) 1/4   (4) 1/16

2. Compared to the half-life and decay mode of the nuclide 90-Sr, the nuclide 226-Ra has
   (1) A longer half-life and the same decay mode
   (2) A longer half-life and a different decay mode
   (3) A shorter half-life and the same decay mode
   (4) A shorter half-life and a different decay mode

3. After decaying for 48 hours, 1/16 of the original mass of a radioisotope sample remains unchanged. What is the half-life of this radioisotope?
   (1) 3.0 h   (3) 12 h
   (2) 9.6 h   (4) 24 h

4. Which nuclide is listed with its half-life and decay mode?
   (1) K-37, 1.24 h, α
   (2) N-16, 7.1 s, β^-
   (3) Rn-222, 1.6×10^3 y, α
   (4) U-235, 7.1×10^8 y, β^-

5. An original sample of K-40 has a mass of 25.00 grams. After 3.9×10^9 years, 3.125 grams of the original sample remains unchanged. What is the half-life of K-40?
   (1) 1.3×10^9 y   (3) 3.9×10^9 y
   (2) 2.6×10^9 y   (4) 1.2×10^{10} y

6. *Compare the penetrating power of beta and gamma emissions.

7. Based on Table N, determine the total time required for an 80.00-gram sample of cobalt-60 to decay until only 10.00 grams of the sample remain unchanged.

Questions 8-10: *When uranium-235 nuclei are bombarded with neutrons, many different combinations of smaller nuclei can be produced. The production of neodymium-150 and germanium-81 in one of these reactions is represented by the equation below.*

$$^{1}_{0}n + ^{235}_{92}U \rightarrow ^{150}_{60}Nd + ^{81}_{32}Ge + 5^{1}_{0}n$$

Germanium-81 and uranium-235 have different decay modes. Ge-81 emits beta particles and has a half-life of 7.6 seconds.

8. *State the number of protons and number of neutrons in a neodymium-150 atom.

9. Complete the following equation for the decay of Ge-81 by writing a notation for the missing nuclide.
   $$^{81}_{32}Ge \rightarrow ^{0}_{-1}e + \underline{\hspace{1cm}}$$

10. Determine the time required for a 16.00-gram sample of Ge-81 to decay until only 1.00 gram of the sample remains unchanged.

Questions 11-12: *The diagram below shows the first three steps in the uranium-238 radioactive decay series. The decay mode for the first and third steps is shown above the arrows. The decay mode for the second step is not shown in the diagram. Thorium-234 has a half-life of 24.10 days.*

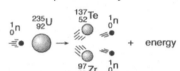

11. *Explain, in terms of neutrons and protons, why U-238 and U-234 are different isotopes of uranium.

12. Identify the decay mode particle emitted from the Th-234.

Questions 13-14: *Nuclear fission reactions can produce different radioisotopes. One of these radioisotopes is Te-137, which has a half-life of 2.5 seconds. The diagram below represents one of the many nuclear fission reactions.*

13. *State evidence that this nuclear reaction represents transmutation.

14. Complete the nuclear equation below for the beta decay of Zr-97, by writing an isotopic notation for the missing product.

$$^{97}_{40}Zr \rightarrow\ ^{0}_{-1}e +\ \underline{\hspace{2cm}}$$

Questions 15-17: *Polonium-210 occurs naturally but is scarce. Polonium-210 is primarily used in devices designed to eliminate static electricity in machinery. It is also used in brushes to remove dust from camera lenses. Polonium-210 can be created in the laboratory by bombarding bismuth-209 with neutrons to create bismuth-210. The bismuth-210 undergoes beta decay to produce polonium-210. Polonium-210 has a half-life of 138 days and undergoes alpha decay.*

15. *State one beneficial use of Po-210.

16. Determine the total mass of an original 28.0-milligram sample of Po-210 that remains unchanged after 414 days.

17. Identify the decay mode of K-37.

Questions 18-19: *The atomic mass and natural abundance of the naturally occuring isotopes of hydrogen are shown in the table below. The isotope H-2, also called deuterium, is usually represented by the symbol "D." Heavy water forms when deuterium reacts with oxygen, producing molecules of D_2O.*

18. *Explain, in terms of subatomic particles, why atoms of H-1, H-2, and H-3 are each electrically neutral.

19. Based on Table N, identify the decay mode of tritium.

Naturally Occuring Isotopes of Hydrogen

Isotope	Common Name of Isotope	Atomic Mass (u)	Natural Abundance (%)
H-1	protium	1.0078	99.9885
H-2	deuterium	2.0141	0.0115
H-3	tritium	3.0160	negligible

NEW YORK STATE
CHEMISTRY REFERENCE TABLES

TABLE P

ORGANIC PREFIXES

Table P
Organic Prefixes

5
on
Tables P, Q, R

Prefix	Number of Carbon Atoms
meth-	1
eth-	2
prop-	3
but-	4
pent-	5
hex-	6
hept-	7
oct-	8
non-	9
dec-	10

TABLE P: Organic Prefixes

Table P lists 10 **prefixes** used in *organic chemistry*, each representing a different number of **carbon atoms**. (See below for a more thorough explanation.)

Organic chemistry → the study of **organic compounds.** Most organic chemistry questions on the regents are based on the following 3 tables (P, Q, R), so it is worth spending time on understanding them well.

Organic compound → a compound that contains **carbon (C)** as part of its makeup. There are many kinds of organic compounds because carbon can bond in many different ways. Most organic molecules are made of a **chain (or continuous line) of carbon atoms** surrounded by **hydrogen** and/or other atoms.

Table P Organic Prefixes	
Prefix	Number of Carbon Atoms
meth-	1
eth-	2
prop-	3
but-	4
pent-	5
hex-	6
hept-	7
oct-	8
non-	9
dec-	10

Reading the Table:

♦ Every organic compound has, within its name, a **PREFIX** that gives you the **NUMBER OF CARBON ATOMS** in the chain that the compound is based on. The first ten prefixes and the numbers they stand for are listed on **Table P.**

♦ Examples:
   → An organic compound called **ethane** would have **2** carbon atoms in its chain, and so would **ethene** and **ethyne**, since they all begin with the prefix *eth-*.
   → A compound called **heptanol** would have **7** carbon atoms within its chain, since it begins with the prefix *hept-*.
   → **Propanamide** - **3** carbon atoms – begins with prefix *prop-*.

♦ Note: There are no regents questions based on this table alone. However, you will refer to this table many times when answering other organic chemistry questions in the upcoming sections.

NEW YORK STATE
CHEMISTRY REFERENCE TABLES

TABLE Q

HOMOLOGOUS SERIES OF HYDROCARBONS

Table Q
Homologous Series of Hydrocarbons

Name	General Formula	Examples	
		Name	Structural Formula
alkanes	C_nH_{2n+2}	ethane	H H │ │ H—C—C—H │ │ H H
alkenes	C_nH_{2n}	ethene	H﹨ ﹪H C=C H﹍ ﹏H
alkynes	C_nH_{2n-2}	ethyne	H—C≡C—H

Note: n = number of carbon atoms

TABLE Q: Homologous Series of Hydrocarbons

Table Q
Homologous Series of Hydrocarbons

Name	General Formula	Examples	
		Name	Structural Formula
alkanes	C_nH_{2n+2}	ethane	$\begin{array}{c} H \quad H \\ | \quad | \\ H-C-C-H \\ | \quad | \\ H \quad H \end{array}$
alkenes	C_nH_{2n}	ethene	$\begin{array}{c} H \qquad H \\ \diagdown \qquad \diagup \\ C=C \\ \diagup \qquad \diagdown \\ H \qquad H \end{array}$
alkynes	C_nH_{2n-2}	ethyne	$H-C\equiv C-H$

Note: *n* = number of carbon atoms

Table Q gives the *general formula* and then *a specific example* of a member of that homologous series of hydrocarbons.

(Homologous series → a group of related compounds whose specific formulas can be figured out from the same general formula)

Hydrocarbon → organic compounds with only **hydrogen (H)** and **carbon (C)** within their structures.

Reading the Table:

♦ The **NAME** column on the *left* gives you the *general* name of the category of hydrocarbons. The second **NAME** column under **EXAMPLES** gives you an example of a *specific molecule* in this category.

➔ A hydrocarbon is named for the **number** of carbon atoms in its main chain *and* for the **type of bonds** between those carbon atoms.

⇨ Carbon can form *single* bonds, *double* bonds and *triple* bonds to become stable.

✓ *Saturated compounds* → compounds containing carbon with only **single** bonds between them – the carbon atoms are "full." (Each carbon atom has 4 bonds total. These carbons are connected to 4 other atoms, so no other atoms can be added.)

✓ *Unsaturated compounds* → organic compounds with **double** bonds or **triple** bonds – they are not "full" – since theoretically, one/both of the "extra" carbon-carbon bonds can be broken to enable another hydrogen atom to attach itself to the molecule.

➔ There are three general categories of hydrocarbons: **alkanes**, **alkenes** and **alkynes**.

⇨ *Alkanes* are **saturated**. There are only *single* bonds between the carbons.

⇨ *Alkenes* are **unsaturated** → it has one *double* bond within its structure.

⇨ *Alkynes* are also **unsaturated** → it has one *triple* bond within its structure.

♦ All the above information can be seen on the table, under the **GENERAL FORMULA** and **EXAMPLES** headings.

➔ The **GENERAL FORMULA** column gives you the general rule for *the proportion of hydrogens to carbons* for each category of hydrocarbon.

⇨ The formula for **alkanes** is C_nH_{2n+2}. This means that for every carbon atom (C) in the chain, there are 2 times that amount plus 2 hydrogen (H) atoms.

✓ An example of this rule is seen on the table – in the **EXAMPLES** column under **STRUCTURAL FORMULA**. The compound shown has **2** carbon atoms in its main chain and (2***2**)+2, or **6**, hydrogen atoms.

☼ An alkane with **5** carbons has **12** hydrogens – (2*5)+2 = 12.

☼ An alkane with **30** carbons has **62** hydrogens – (2*30)+2 = 62.

✓You can also see on the structural formula that there is only a **single bond** between the carbon atoms, which makes the compound *saturated*. It is "full" – since the carbon atoms are each bonded with four other atoms, nothing else can be added to this compound.

✓The **NAME** of the compound shown is *ethane* because, as stated above, hydrocarbons are named for the **number** of carbon atoms they contain *and* for the **type of bonds** between these atoms.

☼ Ethane contains *two* carbon atoms, so its name begins with the prefix *eth-*. (See Table P – Organic Prefixes.)

☼ Ethane only contains *single* bonds between its carbon atoms, following the alkane rule, so its name ends with *-ane*.

☼ Following the above pattern, a hydrocarbon with only single bonds containing **7** carbon atoms in the chain would be named *heptane* → **hept-** for the *7 carbons* and **-ane** because it is an *alkane* – contains only *single* bonds.

Table P Organic Prefixes	
Prefix	Number of Carbon Atoms
meth-	1
eth-	2
prop-	3
but-	4
pent-	5
hex-	6
hept-	7
oct-	8
non-	9
dec-	10

Carbon Bonding Patterns

Since carbon has four valence electrons, it needs four bonds to gain a full valence shell and become stable. (When drawing a structural formula for an organic compound, always ensure that carbon has four "lines" – representing bonds coming out of it.)

Carbon can bond in four ways:

1. It can form *four* single bonds, in which case it is *saturated*
2. *two* single bonds and *one* double bond (*unsaturated*)
3. *one* single bond and *one* triple bond (*unsaturated*)
4. *two* double bonds (*unsaturated*)

⇨ The formula for **alkenes** is C_nH_{2n}. This means that for every carbon atom (C) in the compound, there are 2 times that amount of hydrogen (H) atoms.

✓ An example of this rule is seen on the table – in the **EXAMPLES** column under **STRUCTURAL FORMULA**. The compound shown has **2** carbon atoms and 2***2**, or **4**, hydrogen atoms.

⚬ An alkene with **5** carbons has **10** hydrogens – 2***5** = 10.

⚬ An alkene with **30** carbons has **60** hydrogens – 2***30** = 60.

✓ See the **double bond** between the two carbon atoms on the example's structural formula. This makes the compound *unsaturated* – since it is not "full" – the extra bond between the two carbons can be broken if necessary so more hydrogen atoms can join the compound.

✓ The **NAME** of the compound shown is *ethene*:

Table P	
Organic Prefixes	
Prefix	Number of Carbon Atoms
meth-	1
eth-	2
prop-	3
but-	4
pent-	5
hex-	6
hept-	7
oct-	8
non-	9
dec-	10

⚬ Ethene contains *two* carbon atoms, so its name begins with the prefix *eth-*. (See Table P – Organic Prefixes.)

⚬ Ethene contains a *double* bond between its carbon atoms, following the **alkene** rule, so its name ends with *-ene*.

⚬ Following the above pattern, a hydrocarbon with one double bond containing **5** carbon atoms in the chain would be named *pentene* → **pent-** for the *5 carbons* and *-ene* because it is an *alkene* – contains a *double* bond.

⇨ The formula for **alkynes** is C_nH_{2n-2}. This means that for every carbon atom (C) in the compound, there are 2 times that amount of hydrogen minus 2 hydrogen (H) atoms.

✓ An example of this rule is seen on the table – in the **EXAMPLES** column under **STRUCTURAL FORMULA**. The compound shown has **2** carbon atoms and (2***2**)-2, or **2**, hydrogen atoms.

$$H-C\equiv C-H$$

⚬ An alkyne with **5** carbons has **8** hydrogens – (2***5**) - 2 = 8.

⚬ An alkyne with **30** carbons has **58** hydrogens – (2***30**) - 2 = 58.

✓ See the **triple** bond on the example's structural formula. This bond makes the compound *unsaturated*.

✓ The **NAME** of the compound shown is *ethyne*:

Table P
Organic Prefixes

Prefix	Number of Carbon Atoms
meth-	1
eth-	2
prop-	3
but-	4
pent-	5
hex-	6
hept-	7
oct-	8
non-	9
dec-	10

⚙ Ethyne contains *two* carbon atoms, so its name begins with the prefix *eth-*. (See **Table P – Organic Prefixes**.)

⚙ Ethene contains a *triple* bond between its carbon atoms, following the **alkyne** rule, so its name ends with *-yne*.

⚙ Following the above pattern, a hydrocarbon with one triple bond containing **3** carbon atoms in the chain would be named *propyne* → **prop-** for the *5 carbons* and **-yne** because it is an *alkyne* – contains a *triple* bond.

More on Naming Hydrocarbons

Alkenes and alkynes can sometimes have a number before their name, such as 2-pentyne, or 3-octene. The number before the hydrocarbon's name tells you after which carbon in the carbon chain the double or triple bond is.

- 2-pentyne: there are 5 Cs, and the triple bond is after the 2nd carbon and before the 3rd. Start counting from the end carbon that is closest to the double or triple bond or functional group. (It doesn't matter which way you start from when drawing the molecule.)
- 3-octene: there are eight Cs, and the double bond is after the 3rd carbon and before the 4th.

---

1. What is the general formula for the homologous series that includes ethene?
   (1) C_nH_{2n} (3) C_nH_{2n-2}
   (2) C_nH_{2n-6} (4) C_nH_{2n+2}

2. Given the formula of a compound:

$$H-C\equiv C-\overset{\overset{H}{|}}{C}-\overset{\overset{H}{|}}{C}-H$$

   This compound is classified as an
   (1) aldehyde   (3) alkyne
   (2) alkene   (4) alcohol

3. Which compound is saturated?
   (1) butane   (3) heptene
   (2) ethene   (4) pentyne

4. Which formula represents an alkyne?
   (1) C_nH_n (3) C_nH_{2n+2}
   (2) $C_{2n}H_n$ (4) C_nH_{2n-2}

5. A molecule of which compound has a multiple covalent bond?
   (1) CH_4 (2) C_2H_4 (3) C_3H_8 (4) C_4H_{10}

6. Which formula can represent an alkyne?
   (1) C_2H_4 (2) C_2H_6 (3) C_3H_4 (4) C_3H_6

7. What is the chemical name for the compound $CH_3CH_2CH_2CH_3$?
   (1) Butane   (3) decane
   (2) Butene   (4) decene

Questions 8 and 9:

$$2\left[H-\overset{\overset{H}{|}}{\underset{\underset{H}{|}}{C}}-\overset{\overset{H}{|}}{\underset{\underset{H}{|}}{C}}-OH\right] \xrightarrow{H_2SO_4} H-\overset{\overset{H}{|}}{\underset{\underset{H}{|}}{C}}-\overset{\overset{H}{|}}{\underset{\underset{H}{|}}{C}}-O-\overset{\overset{H}{|}}{\underset{\underset{H}{|}}{C}}-\overset{\overset{H}{|}}{\underset{\underset{H}{|}}{C}}-H + H_2O$$

Compound A   Compound B

8. *Identify the element in Compound B that makes it an organic compound.

9. Explain, in terms of elements, why Compound B is not a hydrocarbon.

My Notes on the Previous Section(s):

NEW YORK STATE
CHEMISTRY REFERENCE TABLES

TABLE R

ORGANIC FUNCTIONAL GROUPS

Table R
Organic Functional Groups

Class of Compound	Functional Group	General Formula	Example
halide (halocarbon)	—F (fluoro-) —Cl (chloro-) —Br (bromo-) —I (iodo-)	$R-X$ (X represents any halogen)	$CH_3CHClCH_3$ 2-chloropropane
alcohol	—OH	$R-OH$	$CH_3CH_2CH_2OH$ 1-propanol
ether	—O—	$R-O-R'$	$CH_3OCH_2CH_3$ methyl ethyl ether
aldehyde	$\overset{O}{\overset{\|\|}{-C-H}}$	$\overset{O}{\overset{\|\|}{R-C-H}}$	$CH_3CH_2\overset{O}{\overset{\|\|}{C}}-H$ propanal
ketone	$\overset{O}{\overset{\|\|}{-C-}}$	$\overset{O}{\overset{\|\|}{R-C-R'}}$	$CH_3\overset{O}{\overset{\|\|}{C}}CH_2CH_2CH_3$ 2-pentanone
organic acid	$\overset{O}{\overset{\|\|}{-C-OH}}$	$\overset{O}{\overset{\|\|}{R-C-OH}}$	$CH_3CH_2\overset{O}{\overset{\|\|}{C}}-OH$ propanoic acid
ester	$\overset{O}{\overset{\|\|}{-C-O-}}$	$\overset{O}{\overset{\|\|}{R-C-O-R'}}$	$CH_3CH_2\overset{O}{\overset{\|\|}{C}}OCH_3$ methyl propanoate
amine	$-\overset{\|}{N}-$	$R-\overset{R'}{\overset{\|}{N}}-R''$	$CH_3CH_2CH_2NH_2$ 1-propanamine
amide	$\overset{O}{\overset{\|\|}{-C-NH}}$	$\overset{O}{\overset{\|\|}{R-C-}}\overset{R'}{\overset{\|}{NH}}$	$CH_3CH_2\overset{O}{\overset{\|\|}{C}}-NH_2$ propanamide

Note: R represents a bonded atom or group of atoms.

TABLE R: Organic Functional Groups

Table R
Organic Functional Groups

Class of Compound	Functional Group	General Formula	Example
halide (halocarbon)	$-F$ (fluoro-) $-Cl$ (chloro-) $-Br$ (bromo-) $-I$ (iodo-)	$R-X$ (X represents any halogen)	$CH_3CHClCH_3$ 2-chloropropane
alcohol	$-OH$	$R-OH$	$CH_3CH_2CH_2OH$ 1-propanol
ether	$-O-$	$R-O-R'$	$CH_3OCH_2CH_3$ methyl ethyl ether
aldehyde	$\overset{O}{\overset{\|}{-C}}-H$	$\overset{O}{\overset{\|}{R-C}}-H$	$CH_3CH_2\overset{O}{\overset{\|}{C}}-H$ propanal
ketone	$\overset{O}{\overset{\|}{-C}}-$	$\overset{O}{\overset{\|}{R-C}}-R'$	$CH_3\overset{O}{\overset{\|}{C}}CH_2CH_2CH_3$ 2-pentanone
organic acid	$\overset{O}{\overset{\|}{-C}}-OH$	$\overset{O}{\overset{\|}{R-C}}-OH$	$CH_3CH_2\overset{O}{\overset{\|}{C}}-OH$ propanoic acid
ester	$\overset{O}{\overset{\|}{-C}}-O-$	$\overset{O}{\overset{\|}{R-C}}-O-R'$	$CH_3CH_2\overset{O}{\overset{\|}{C}}OCH_3$ methyl propanoate
amine	$-\overset{\|}{N}-$	$R-\overset{\overset{R'}{\|}}{N}-R''$	$CH_3CH_2CH_2NH_2$ 1-propanamine
amide	$\overset{O}{\overset{\|}{-C}}-\overset{\|}{N}H$	$R-\overset{O}{\overset{\|}{C}}-\overset{\overset{R'}{\|}}{N}H$	$CH_3CH_2\overset{O}{\overset{\|}{C}}-NH_2$ propanamide

Note: R represents a bonded atom or group of atoms.

Table R lists **9 categories of organic compounds** (other than hydrocarbons), their **functional groups**, their **general formulas** and specific **examples** of each one.

Functional group → a specific element or a group of bonded elements that replaces a hydrogen in a hydrocarbon, causing it to lose its hydrocarbon classification and become a different class of organic compound. The functional group is what gives each class of organic compound its **specific unique properties**.

Reading the Table:

An Overview of the Table:

♦ The first column from the left gives you the name of the new **CLASS OF COMPOUND** being formed when the **FUNCTIONAL GROUP**, listed in the second column, is added to the hydrocarbon. You can see in the **FUNCTIONAL GROUP** column whether the group will be located somewhere in the middle of the compound or at its end, based on the lines (representing bonds) sticking out of the functional group.

➔ For example, for an organic compound to be classified as a *halide/halocarbon*, it must contain either **fluorine (F)**, **chlorine (Cl)**, **bromine (Br)** or **iodine (I)**. There is only one line/bond sticking out of each group. This means that it makes one bond and therefore will replace a hydrogen connected to a carbon.

halide (halocarbon)	— F (fluoro-) — Cl (chloro-) — Br (bromo-) — I (iodo-)

♦ The **GENERAL FORMULA** column looks very similar to the **FUNCTIONAL GROUP** column.

➔ The **GENERAL FORMULA** column only adds the *"R"*s representing atoms or groups of atoms (as seen in the note under the table) attached to the functional group, showing that there's more to the compound than simply the group shown in the table.

➔ For all practical purposes, it is enough to look at only one of the two above columns when using this table.

♦ The **EXAMPLE** column gives you a specific example for each **CLASS OF COMPOUND**, with both its structural formula written out and its name. This information can help you figure out how to draw or name another type of this compound.

A Detailed Look at the Table:

♦ **Halides/Halocarbons:**

halide (halocarbon)	—F (fluoro-) —Cl (chloro-) —Br (bromo-) —I (iodo-)	R—X (X represents any halogen)	$CH_3CHCICH_3$ 2-chloropropane

→ **FUNCTIONAL GROUP:** either **F**, **Cl**, **Br** or **I** bonded to one C atom within the chain. As seen in the **FUNCTIONAL GROUP** and **GENERAL FORMULA** columns, the functional group will not bond with 2 carbons at the same time, since each of them only need one bond to become stable. A halide may have *more than one functional group*, each bonded to a carbon atom.

→ An **EXAMPLE** of a halide is $CH_3CHCICH_3$, or **2-chloropropane**.

⇨ $CH_3CHCICH_3$ is the **structural formula**, which tells you exactly how to *draw* the compound:

✓ First, draw one C with 3 Hs coming out of that C.

✓ Then draw another C with a H and a Cl coming out of that C. It doesn't matter whether the Cl is on the top or the bottom.

✓ Then another C with 3 Hs coming out of that C. All done 😊

⇨ The *name* of the compound is **2-chloropropane**. Why? Taking it step-by-step, starting from the end:

✓ The compound's name ends in **-ane** because it used to be part of the alk**ane** family – a hydrocarbon with only single bonds between the carbons. (Table Q – Series of Hydrocarbons)

✓ *Prop-* because there are 3 carbons in the chain. (Table P – Organic Prefixes)

✓ *Chloro-* because its functional group is **chlorine (Cl)**. (The second column on the table informs you that the prefix for F is *flouro-*; Cl is *chloro-* etc.) The chlorine replaced a hydrogen atom in the alkane and turned it into a halide, with its unique properties. Note that halide functional groups are written before the name of the main chain.

✓ *2-* to let you know the **exact position** of the functional group, in this case, the *chlorine*. It is attached to the *second* carbon. In this case, it is the second carbon from both the right and the left, but generally, when assigning a number, start from the side that gives you the smaller number.

Ex 1: *Draw* **3-bromo, 4-iodooctane** *and give its* *structural formula*.

➜ Use the compound's *name* to figure out how it looks.

⇨ *Octane* → 8 carbons singly bonded to one another, with hydrogens bonded to the carbons in every available position. (Some hydrogens will be replaced – see below.)

⇨ *4-iodo* → 1 iodine (I) bonded to the 4th carbon (replacing a hydrogen)

⇨ *3-bromo* → 1 bromine (Br) bonded to the 3rd carbon (replacing a hydrogen)

➜ For **the structural formula:** Looking at your drawing, begin with a C, (usually) going from l→r:

⇨ First there's a C with 3 Hs bonded to it → **CH_3**.

⇨ Then C with 2 Hs → CH_3**CH_2**

⇨ C with H and Br → CH_3CH_2**$CHBr$**

⇨ C with H and I → CH_3CH_2CHBr**CHI**

⇨ C with 2 Hs... 3 times, then C with 3 Hs → $CH_3CH_2CHBrCHI$**$CH_2CH_2CH_2CH_3$**
(this compound can also be written as $CH_3CH_2CHBrCHI$**$(CH_2)_3$**CH_3)

Ex 2: *Name* the molecule below:

➜ I see Cl and F, so I know it is a halide/halocarbon – so its name will end in **-ane**.

➜ It has 4 Cs, so its name is **butane**.

➜ It has 2 Cls, both in the second position from the left → **2, 2 di-chloro,** butane. (*di-* means two)

➜ It has 1 F in the 3rd position from the left → **3-fluoro,** *2, 2-di-chlorobutane*.

◆ *Alcohols*:

alcohol	—OH	R—OH	$CH_3CH_2CH_2OH$ 1-propanol

➔ **FUNCTIONAL GROUP: OH** → an oxygen atom bonded to a hydrogen atom. As seen in the **FUNCTIONAL GROUP** and **GENERAL FORMULA** columns, the OH group can only be attached to one carbon. (It cannot be in between 2 carbons, since hydrogen can only bond with one other atom and it is already bonded to the oxygen.)

➔ An **EXAMPLE** of an alcohol is $CH_3CH_2CH_2OH$, or *1-propanol*.

⇨ $CH_3CH_2CH_2OH$ is the **structural formula**:

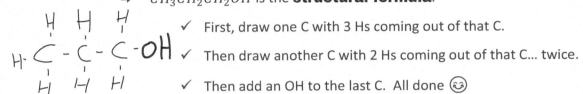

✓ First, draw one C with 3 Hs coming out of that C.

✓ Then draw another C with 2 Hs coming out of that C... twice.

✓ Then add an OH to the last C. All done ☺

⇨ The *name* of the compound is **1-propanol**. Why?

✓ The compound's name ends in **-ol** because it is an alcoh**ol**, meaning it contains the OH functional group. It is -**an**ol because there are single bonds (alk**ane**) between all the Cs.

✓ *Prop-* because it has 3 carbons in the chain. (Table P – Organic Prefixes)

✓ **1-** to let you know the **exact position** of the functional group, the *OH*. It is attached to the *first* carbon. (Always count from side that will give you a lower number – doesn't matter whether right or left.)

Ex 1: *Draw* **2-butanol** *and give its structural formula.*

➔ Use the compound's *name* to figure out how it looks.

⇨ It ends in *-ol,* so it is an *alcohol.* Therefore, it must have an OH group somewhere.

⇨ *But-* means it has 4 carbons.

⇨ 2- → The OH group is bonded to the 2nd carbon.

➔ The structural formula:

⇨ First there's a C with 3 Hs bonded to it → *CH₃*.

⇨ Then C with 2 Hs → *CH₃CH₂*

⇨ C with H and OH → *CH₃CH₂CHOH* (The Hs don't combine to H₂ since the 2nd H is part of the functional group.)

⇨ C with 3 Hs → *CH₃CH₂CHOHCH₃*

Ex 2: *Name the molecule below:*

➔ I see the OH functional group, so I know it is an alcohol – so its name will end in -*anol*.

➔ It has 5 Cs, so its name is *pentanol*.

➔ The functional group is 3rd → **3-pentanol**.

- **Ethers:**

ether	—O—	R—O—R′	$CH_3OCH_2CH_3$ methyl ethyl ether

➔ **FUNCTIONAL GROUP: O** → an oxygen atom. As seen in the **FUNCTIONAL GROUP** and **GENERAL FORMULA** columns, this O must bond with 2 carbons – one on either side of it.

➔ An **EXAMPLE** of an ether is $CH_3OCH_2CH_3$, or **methyl ethyl ether**.

⇨ $CH_3OCH_2CH_3$ is the **structural formula**:

✓ First, draw one C with 3 Hs.

✓ Then draw an O bonded to that C on the other side.

✓ Then a C with 2 Hs, then a C with 3 Hs. All done 😊

> Lines coming out of carbon atoms in an organic molecule (as in the diagrams below) represent bonded hydrogen atoms. It isn't necessary to draw the Hs.

⇨ The *name* of the compound is **methyl ethyl ether**. Why?

✓ The compound's name ends in **ether** because it is an **ether**, meaning it contains the -O- functional group.

✓ **Methyl** and **ethyl** are both names of *alkyl* groups → a group of bonded carbon and hydrogen atoms "sticking out" of a compound (or "an alkane missing a hydrogon atom"). A methyl group has 1 carbon atom and ethyl group has 2 carbon atoms. (**Table P – Organic Prefixes**) In this compound, moving from l→r and focusing on the functional group (O), we see that there is a methyl group to its left and an ethyl group to its right.

Example 1: *Draw* **propyl butyl ether** *and give its structural formula.*

➔ Use the compound's *name* to figure out how it looks.

⇨ It ends in *ether,* so it is an *ether*. Therefore, it must have an O somewhere in the chain of carbons, between two carbons.

⇨ *Propyl* means an alkyl group with 3 Cs is on one side of the O.

⇨ *Butyl* means an alkyl group with 4 Cs is on the other side of the O.

➔ The structural formula:

⇨ First there's a C with 3 Hs bonded to it, then C with 2 Hs... twice → $CH_3CH_2CH_2$

⇨ Then O → $CH_3CH_2CH_2O$

⇨ C with 2Hs... 3 times, then C with 3 Hs → $CH_3CH_2CH_2OH_2H_2H_2H_3$ / $CH_3CH_2CH_2O(H_2)_3H_3$

Ex 2: *Name the molecule below:*

➔ I see O bonded to 2 Cs, so I know it is an ether – so its name will end in **ether**.

➔ There are 5 Cs with Hs (*pentyl* group) after the O → **pentyl** ether

➔ There's 1 C with Hs (*methyl* group) before the O → **methyl** pentyl ether.

• **Aldehydes:**

aldehyde	$\begin{matrix} O \\ \| \\ -C-H \end{matrix}$	$\begin{matrix} O \\ \| \\ R-C-H \end{matrix}$	$\begin{matrix} O \\ \| \\ CH_3CH_2C-H \\ \text{propanal} \end{matrix}$

➔ **FUNCTIONAL GROUP: O** double bonded to **C** that's bonded to **H**. As seen in the **FUNCTIONAL GROUP** and **GENERAL FORMULA** columns, this group will be at the end of a chain.

➔ An **EXAMPLE** of an aldehyde is CH_3CH_2CHO (the O can also be represented as double bonded to the C on top, as seen on the table), or **propanal**. (To distinguish at aldehyde from an alcohol in a structural formula, the aldehyde is written <u>C</u>HO – not CH_2<u>O</u>H, which would be an alcohol.)

⇨ CH_3CH_2CHO is the **structural formula**:

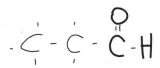

✓ First, draw one C with 3 Hs. Then a C with 2 Hs.

✓ Then another C with an O double bonded to it on top and an H bonded on the right. All done 😊

⇨ The *name* of the compound is **propanal**. Why?

✓ The compound's name ends in -**al** because it is an **al**dehyde, meaning it contains the O=C-H functional group.

✓ **Prop -** → there are 3 Cs in the chain. **(Table P – Organic Prefixes)**

Ex 1: *Draw* **ethanal** *and give its structural formula.*

➔ Use the compound's name to figure out how it looks.

⇨ It ends in *al,* so it is an *aldehyde.* Therefore, it must have an O=C-H group at the end of the chain.

⇨ *Eth-* means 2 Cs, including the C in the functional group.

➔ The structural formula:

⇨ First there's a C with 3 Hs bonded to it → *CH₃*

⇨ Then C double bonded to an O and single bonded to an H → *CH₃CHO*

Ex 2: *Name the molecule below:*

➔ I see the O=C-H functional group, so I know it is an aldehyde – so its name will end in -*al*.

➔ All the bonds between the carbon atoms are single, so it will be -*anal*.

➔ There are 4 Cs in the chain → *butanal*

♦ **Ketones**:

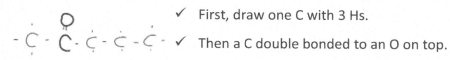

| ketone | $\begin{matrix} O \\ \parallel \\ -C- \end{matrix}$ | $\begin{matrix} O \\ \parallel \\ R-C-R' \end{matrix}$ | $\begin{matrix} O \\ \parallel \\ CH_3CCH_2CH_2CH_3 \\ \text{2-pentanone} \end{matrix}$ |

➔ **FUNCTIONAL GROUP: O** double bonded to **C**. As seen in the **FUNCTIONAL GROUP** and **GENERAL FORMULA** columns, this group will be in the middle of a carbon chain, with a C on both sides.

➔ An **EXAMPLE** of a ketone is $CH_3COCCH_2CH_3$ (the O can also be represented as double bonded to the C on top, as seen on the table), or **2-pentanone**.

⇨ $CH_3COCH_2CH_2CH_3$ is the **structural formula**:

✓ First, draw one C with 3 Hs.

✓ Then a C double bonded to an O on top.

✓ Then a C with 2 Hs... twice, then a C with 3 Hs. All done 😊

⇨ The *name* of the compound is **2-pentanone**. Why?

✓ The compound's name ends in **-one** because it is a ket**one**, meaning it contains the O=C functional group.

✓ **Pent-** → there are 5 Cs in the chain. (**Table P – Organic Prefixes**)

✓ **2-** → the functional group (O=C) is 2nd in the chain of carbons.

Ex 1: *Draw* **propanone** *and give its* *structural formula.*

➔ Use the compound's *name* to figure out how it looks.

⇨ It ends in *-one*, so it is a ketone. Therefore, it must have an O=C group in middle of the C chain.

⇨ *Prop-* means 3 Cs, including the C in the functional group.

⇨ There is no number before the compound's name because there is only one possible place for the functional group to be – since it cannot be at the end of a chain.

➔ The structural formula:

⇨ First there's a C with 3 Hs bonded to it → CH_3

⇨ Then C double bonded to an O → CH_3CO

⇨ Then C with 3 Hs → CH_3COCH_3

Ex 2:

Name the molecule below:

➔ I see the O=C functional group, so I know it is a ketone – so its name will end in *-one*.

➔ The bonds between the carbons are all single, so it will be *-anone*.

➔ There are 6 Cs in the chain → *hexanone*

➔ The functional group is 3rd in the chain → **3-hexanone**

• **Organic acids:**

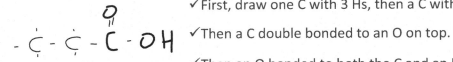

organic acid	$\begin{matrix} O \\ \| \\ -C-OH \end{matrix}$	$\begin{matrix} O \\ \| \\ R-C-OH \end{matrix}$	$\begin{matrix} O \\ \| \\ CH_3CH_2C-OH \\ \text{propanoic acid} \end{matrix}$

→ **FUNCTIONAL GROUP: C** double bonded to **O** and single bonded to **OH** (O bonded to H). As seen in the **FUNCTIONAL GROUP** and **GENERAL FORMULA** columns, this group will be at the end of a carbon chain.

→ An **EXAMPLE** of an organic acid is CH_3CH_2COOH (the O can also be represented as double bonded to the C on top, as seen on the table), or **propanoic acid.**

⇨ CH_3CH_2COOH is the **structural formula:**

$$-\overset{\cdot}{\underset{\cdot}{C}}-\overset{\cdot}{\underset{\cdot}{C}}-\overset{O}{\overset{\|}{C}}-OH$$

✓ First, draw one C with 3 Hs, then a C with 2 Hs.

✓ Then a C double bonded to an O on top.

✓ Then an O bonded to both the C and an H. All done ☺

⇨ The *name* of the compound is **propanoic acid**. Why?

✓ The compound's name ends in *-oic acid* because it is an orga**nic acid**, meaning it contains the O=C-OH functional group.

✓ *prop-* → there are 3 Cs in the chain. (**Table P – Organic Prefixes**)

Ex 1:

Draw **ethanoic acid** *and give its* structural formula.

→ Use the compound's name to figure out how it looks.

⇨ It ends in *-oic acid,* so it is an *organic acid.* Therefore, it must have an O=C-OH group at the end of the C chain.

⇨ *eth-* means 2 Cs, including the C in the functional group.

$$-\overset{\cdot}{\underset{\cdot}{C}}-\overset{O}{\overset{\|}{C}}-OH$$

→ The structural formula:

⇨ First there's a C with 3 Hs bonded to it → CH_3

⇨ Then C double bonded to an O → CH_3CO

⇨ Then an O bonded to an H → CH_3COOH

Ex 2:

Name the molecule below:

$$-\overset{\cdot}{\underset{\cdot}{C}}-\overset{\cdot}{\underset{\cdot}{C}}-\overset{\cdot}{\underset{\cdot}{C}}-\overset{\cdot}{\underset{\cdot}{C}}-\overset{\cdot}{\underset{\cdot}{C}}-\overset{O}{\overset{\|}{C}}-OH$$

→ I see the O=C-OH functional group, so I know it is an organic acid– so its name will end in *-oic acid*.

→ The bonds between the carbons are all single, so it is *-anoic acid*.

→ There are 6 Cs in the chain, including the C in the functional group → **hex**anoic acid

---

◆ **Esters:**

ester	$\begin{matrix} O \\ \| \\ -C-O- \end{matrix}$	$\begin{matrix} O \\ \| \\ R-C-O-R' \end{matrix}$	$\begin{matrix} O \\ \| \\ CH_3CH_2COCH_3 \\ \text{methyl propanoate} \end{matrix}$

➔ **FUNCTIONAL GROUP: C** double bonded to **O** and single bonded to another **O**. As seen in the **FUNCTIONAL GROUP** and **GENERAL FORMULA** columns, this group will be in the middle of a carbon chain.

➔ An **EXAMPLE** of an ester is $CH_3CH_2COOCH_3$ (the first O can also be represented as double bonded to the C on top, as seen on the table), or *methyl propanoate.*

⇨ $CH_3CH_2COOCH_3$ is the **structural formula:**

✓ First, draw one C with 3 Hs, then a C with 2 Hs.

✓ Then C double bonded to an O on top and single bonded to another O

✓ Then a C with 3 Hs. All done 😊

⇨ The *name* of the compound is **methyl propanoate**. Why?

✓ *prop-* → there are 3 Cs *up until and including* the C in the functional group. (Table P – Organic Prefixes)

✓ *methyl* → there is a methyl (1 C) group *after* the functional group.

Ex 1: *Draw* **propyl ethanoate** and give its *structural formula.*

➔ Use the compound's *name* to figure out how it looks.

⇨ It ends in *-oate*, so it is an ester. Therefore, it must have an O=C-O group in the C chain.

⇨ *eth-*→ there are 2 Cs up until and including the C in the functional group

⇨ *propyl* → there's a propyl group (3 Cs) after the functional group

➔ The structural formula:

⇨ First there's a C with 3 Hs bonded to it → *CH₃*

⇨ Then C double bonded to an O and single bonded to another O → *CH₃COO*

⇨ Then C with 2 Hs... twice, then C with 3 Hs → *CH₃COOCH₂CH₂CH₃*

Ex 2: *Name* the molecule below:

➔ I see the O=C-O functional group, so I know it is an ester – so its name will end in *-oate*.

➔ The bonds between the carbons are all single, so it is *-anoate*.

➔ There are 5 Cs *up until and including* the C in the functional group → *pentanoate*

➔ There is a butyl (4 Cs) group *after* the functional group → *butyl* pentanoate

---

◆ **Amines:**

amine	$-\overset{\displaystyle |}{\underset{\displaystyle |}{N}}-$	$R-\overset{\displaystyle R'}{\underset{\displaystyle |}{N}}-R''$	$CH_3CH_2CH_2NH_2$ 1-propanamine

→ **FUNCTIONAL GROUP: N**. As seen in the **FUNCTIONAL GROUP** and **GENERAL FORMULA** columns, an amine is based on an ammonia molecule: NH_3. Either 1, 2 or 3 of the Hs are replaced with a carbon chain (an alkyl group). In this course, it's usually only 1 H that's replaced.

→ An **EXAMPLE** of an amine is $CH_3CH_2CH_2NH_2$, or **1-propanamine.**

⇨ $CH_3CH_2CH_2NH_2$ is the **structural formula**:

✓ First, draw one C with 3 Hs, then a C with 2 Hs… twice.

✓ Then a N with 2 Hs. All done ☺

$$-\overset{|}{\underset{|}{C}}-\overset{|}{\underset{|}{C}}-\overset{|}{\underset{|}{C}}-N-$$

⇨ The *name* of the compound is **1-propanamine**. Why?

✓ The compound's name ends in **-amine** because it is an **amine**, meaning it contains the N functional group.

✓ **prop-** → there are 3 Cs in the chain that replace the Hs with single bonds between all the carbons in the chain. (**Table P – Organic Prefixes**)

✓ **1-** → the functional group is 1st in the chain.

Ex 1: *Draw* **1-heptanamine** *and give its structural formula.*

→ Use the compound's *name* to figure out how it looks.

⇨ It ends in *-amine,* so it is an *amine.* Therefore, it must have a N somewhere along the C chain.

⇨ *hept-*→there are 7 Cs $N-\overset{|}{\underset{|}{C}}-\overset{|}{\underset{|}{C}}-\overset{|}{\underset{|}{C}}-\overset{|}{\underset{|}{C}}-\overset{|}{\underset{|}{C}}-\overset{|}{\underset{|}{C}}-\overset{|}{\underset{|}{C}}-$

⇨ *1-* → the functional group is 1st in the chain

→ The structural formula:

⇨ First there's a N with 3 Hs bonded to it → NH_3

⇨ Then 6 Cs with 2Hs bonded to them → $NH_3CH_2CH_2CH_2CH_2CH_2CH_2$

⇨ Then a C with 3 Hs → $NH_3CH_2CH_2CH_2CH_2CH_2CH_2CH_3$ or $NH_3(CH_2)_6CH_3$

Ex 2: *Name the molecule below:*

$-\overset{|}{\underset{|}{C}}-\overset{|}{\underset{|}{C}}-\overset{|}{\underset{|}{C}}-\overset{|}{\underset{|}{C}}-\overset{|}{\underset{|}{C}}-\overset{|}{\underset{|}{C}}-\overset{|}{\underset{|}{C}}-\overset{|}{\underset{|}{C}}-N-$

→ I see the N functional group, so I know it is an amine – its name will end in *-amine.*

→ The bonds between the Cs are all single, so it is - *an*amine.

→ There are 8 Cs → *octanamine*

→ The functional group is 1st in the chain (count from the side that gives you a smaller number) → *1-octanamine*

♦ **Amides**:

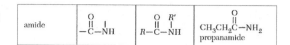

amide	$\begin{matrix} O \\ \parallel \\ -C-NH \end{matrix}$	$\begin{matrix} O \quad R' \\ \parallel \quad \mid \\ R-C-NH \end{matrix}$	$\begin{matrix} O \\ \parallel \\ CH_3CH_2C-NH_2 \\ \text{propanamide} \end{matrix}$

➜ **FUNCTIONAL GROUP: C** double bonded to **O** and single bonded to **NH**. As seen in the **FUNCTIONAL GROUP** and **GENERAL FORMULA** columns, the functional group will at the end of a carbon chain.

➜ An **EXAMPLE** of an amide is $CH_3CH_2CONH_2$, or **propanamide.**

⇨ $CH_3CH_2CONH_2$ is the **structural formula**:

✓ First, draw one C with 3 Hs, then a C with 2 Hs.

✓ Then a C double bonded to an O.

✓ Then a N bonded to 2 Hs. All done 😊

⇨ The *name* of the compound is **propanamide**. Why?

✓ The compound's name ends in **-amide** because it is an **amide**, meaning it contains the O=C-NH functional group.

✓ **prop-** → there are 3 Cs in the chain. (**Table P – Organic Prefixes**)

Ex 1:

Draw **butanamide** *and give its* *structural formula*.

➜ Use the compound's *name* to figure out how it looks.

⇨ It ends in *-amide,* so it is an *amide*. Therefore, it must have an O=C-NH group at the end of the C chain.

⇨ *but-* → there are 4 Cs

➜ The structural formula:

⇨ First there's a C with 3 Hs bonded to it, then C with 2 Hs... twice → $CH_3CH_2CH_2$

⇨ Then a C double bonded to an O → CH_3CH_2CO

⇨ Then a NH bonded to another H → $CH_3CH_2CONH_2$

Ex 2:

Name the molecule below:

➜ I see the O=C-NH functional group, so I know it is an amide – so it will end in *-amide*.

➜ The bonds between the Cs are all single, so it will be *-anamide*.

➜ There are 2 Cs → *ethanamide*

1. Given the formula representing a molecule:

H H H H H
| | | | |
H−C−C−C−C−C−N
| | | | | ╱H
H H H H H   ╲H

A chemical name for this compound is

(1) pentanone   (3) 1-pentanamine

(2) 1-pentanol   (4) pentanamide

2. Given the formula:

H H H H
| | | |
H−C−C−C−C−N
| | | | ╱H
H H H H   ╲H

What is a chemical name of this compound?

(1) 1-butanamide   (3) 1-butanamine
(2) 4-butanamide   (4) 4-butanamine

3. *A molecule of any organic compound has at least one

(1) ionic bond   (3) oxygen atom
(2) double bond   (4) carbon atom

4. Amines, amides, and amino acids are categories of

(1) Isomers
(2) organic compounds
(3) isotopes
(4) inorganic compounds

5. *An alcohol and an ether have the same molecular formula, C_2H_6O. These two compounds have

(1) the same functional group and the same physical and chemical properties
(2) the same functional group and different physical and chemical properties
(3) different functional groups and the same physical and chemical properties
(4) different functional groups and different physical and chemical properties

6. Draw a structural formula for methanal.

7. *Draw a structural formula for 2-butanol.

Questions 8 and 9:
Ethyl ethanoate is used as a solvent for varnishes and in the manufacture of artificial leather. The formula below represents a molecule of ethyl ethanoate.

H O   H H
| ‖ | |
H−C−C−O−C−C−H
| | |
H   H H

8. *Identify the element in ethyl ethanoate that makes it an organic compound.

9. Write the name of the class of organic compounds to which this compound belongs.

10. *The equation below represents an industrial preparation of diethyl ether.*

$$2\left(H-\underset{\underset{H}{|}}{\overset{\overset{H}{|}}{C}}-\underset{\underset{H}{|}}{\overset{\overset{H}{|}}{C}}-OH\right) \xrightarrow{H_2SO_4} H-\underset{\underset{H}{|}}{\overset{\overset{H}{|}}{C}}-\underset{\underset{H}{|}}{\overset{\overset{H}{|}}{C}}-O-\underset{\underset{H}{|}}{\overset{\overset{H}{|}}{C}}-\underset{\underset{H}{|}}{\overset{\overset{H}{|}}{C}}-H + H_2O$$

Compound A　　　　　　　**Compound B**

Write the name of the class of organic compounds to which compound A belongs.

11. *Methanol can be manufactured by a reaction that is reversible. In the reaction, carbon monoxide gas and hydrogen gas react using a catalyst. The equation below represents this system at equilibrium.*

$$CO(g) + 2H_2(g) \Leftrightarrow CH_3OH(g) + energy$$

State the class of organic compounds to which the product of the forward reaction belongs.

12. *Fatty acids, a class of compounds found in living things, are organic acids with long hydrocarbon chains. Linoleic acid, an unsaturated fatty acid, is essential for human skin flexibility and smoothness. The formula below represents a molecule of linoleic acid.*

On the diagram above, circle the organic acid functional group.

13. The equation below represents the reaction between 2-methylpropene and hydrogen chloride gas.

Identify the class of organic compounds to which the product belongs.

My Notes on the Previous Section(s):

_____
_____
_____
_____
_____
_____
_____
_____
_____
_____
_____
_____
_____
_____
_____
_____
_____
_____
_____
_____
_____
_____
_____
_____
_____
_____

NEW YORK STATE
CHEMISTRY REFERENCE TABLES

THE

PERIODIC TABLE

OF THE ELEMENTS

[AND SOME OF TABLE S]

Periodic Table of the Elements

Table S
Properties of Selected Elements

16
on
PT, Table S

THE PERIODIC TABLE OF THE ELEMENTS

Periodic Table of the Elements

KEY

Atomic Mass → 12.011

Symbol → **C**

Atomic Number → 6
Electron Configuration → 2-4

Selected Oxidation States → -4 +2 +4

Relative atomic masses are based on $^{12}C = 12$ (exact)

Note: Numbers in parentheses are mass numbers of the most stable or common isotope.

*denotes the presence of (2-8-) for elements 72 and above

**The systematic names and symbols for elements of atomic numbers 113 and above will be used until the approval of trivial names by IUPAC.

Source: *CRC Handbook of Chemistry and Physics*, 91st ed., 2010–2011, CRC Press

Reference Tables for Physical Setting/Chemistry – 2011 Edition

9

The Periodic Table of the Elements is the basis of the entire chemistry course. It lists 118 **elements** along with basic information about each one. Table S supplements the Periodic Table by providing additional information about some of the elements.

➔ *Atom* → the smallest building block of matter that still retains its properties

➔ *Element* → a substance made up of only one type of atom that cannot be decomposed in a chemical reaction

<u>Note:</u> Throughout this book, the abbreviation **PT** stands for **The Periodic Table of the Elements**.

Reading the Table (Part I):

Note the **KEY** on the *top middle* of the PT:

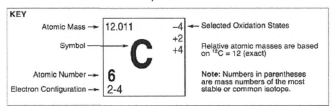

♦ The large **bold** letter in the *center* is the element's *symbol*. Every element has its own 1-2 letter symbol, used when writing chemical formulas containing the element. For example, *H* stands for *hydrogen*, and *O* stands for *oxygen*. A compound with the formula **H₂O** contains 2 atoms of hydrogen and 1 atom of oxygen.

➔ <u>Note:</u> Elements with *2-letter symbols* (ex: calcium – **Ca**) should always have their first letter capitalized and second letter lowercased. Capitalizing both letters on the regents will cause you to lose points!

➔ Use Table S to figure out what each symbol stands for. Use the element's atomic number – the small bold number on the bottom left – to look up the element on Table S. The **C** in the **KEY** stands for carbon.

➔ Sometimes, an element's symbol seems to have no correlation to its actual name. (Because it's related to its Latin name instead.) For example, *Hg* (#80) stands for *mercury*, and *Sb* stands for *antimony*. Therefore, when answering regents questions, unless you are sure you know what the symbol stands for, look it up on Table S.

♦ The small **bold** number on the *bottom left* is the element's *atomic number*. This number tells you how many **protons** each atom of this element contains. All atoms of the same element have the same unique number of protons, which is what gives the element its unique properties.

➔ Unbonded atoms have an *equal number of protons and electrons*. So, in essence, the atomic number also tells you how many **electrons** this atom has. We say it's the number of protons because that number will always remain constant, while the number of an atom's electrons constantly varies – depending on whether and/or how it bonded.

➔ The **6** on the **KEY** tells you that one atom of carbon contains 6 protons and 6 electrons.

♦ The number on the *upper left* is the element's ***atomic mass*** → the *average mass of all naturally occurring isotopes of the element*. Let's take this definition slowly:

➔ Atoms contain **protons, neutrons** and **electrons**. Protons and neutrons each have a mass of 1 amu (atomic mass unit). Electrons have a mass of 1/1836 amu, but since this mass is so small, electrons are considered to have a mass of 0 for all practical purposes. Therefore, when calculating an atom's **mass**, *add its protons and neutrons*.

⇨ For example, if a carbon atom contained **6** protons and **4** neutrons, its mass would be **10**.

➔ As stated above, all atoms of a single element will have the same number of protons. However, the number of neutrons will vary within atoms of the same element. Atoms of the same element with different amounts of neutrons are called **isotopes** of the element.

⇨ For example, K-39 and K-42 are two isotopes of potassium. K-39 has a mass of 39 and K-42 has a mass of 42.

➔ To figure out how many neutrons an atom has, subtract its number of protons from its given mass (mass number), since protons + neutrons = mass number.

⇨ <u>Ex:</u> What is the total number of neutrons in an atom of K-39?

    (1) 19   (3) 21

    (2) 20   (4) 39

⇨ The 39 in "K-39" represents potassium's mass number – the sum of its neutrons and protons. As seen on the PT, potassium has an atomic number of 19 → 19 protons. <u>Subtract:</u> 39 – 19 = **20**. The correct answer is choice 2.

➔ An element's ***atomic mass*** is the **weighted average** of the mass of all the naturally occurring (not artificially produced) isotopes of the element.

➔ **Weighted average** → an average that takes the *relative abundance* of each item into account.

⇨ Meaning, if C with a mass of 12.5 is found 83% of the time, and C with a mass of 10 is found 17% of the time, the atomic mass will not be 11.25, the simple average of the two masses.

⇨ Rather, the following formula is used: Mass of isotope A <u>times</u> relative abundance (percent) of isotope A <u>plus</u> mass of isotope B <u>times</u> relative abundance of isotope B (percent).

⇨ In our example, this would mean multiplying 12.5 by 0.83 and multiplying 10 by 0.17 and then adding the products, resulting in an atomic mass of **12.075**.

♦ The numbers on the *bottom left* represent the element's ***electron configuration*** → how the element's electrons are *arranged* within its atoms.

➜ Electrons are found in **principal energy levels AKA shells** surrounding the nucleus.

⇨ The *closer* the shell is to the nucleus, the *less energy* its electrons have (and v.v.).

⇨ The *lower energy* shells generally get *filled first*. (See below for an exception.)

➜ Each shell can hold *a specific number of electrons*, depending on its distance from the nucleus.

⇨ The *further away* from the nucleus, the *more electrons* a shell can hold.

➜ As seen on the table:

⇨ Shell 1 can hold max **2** electrons.

⇨ Shell 2 can hold max **8** electrons.

✓ Elements 72 and above seem to have first shells with 18 electrons. However, if you look closely, there's a dash before the 18, which represents the standard (2-8-) for the first two shells.

⇨ Shell 3 can hold max **18** electrons.

⇨ Shell 4 can hold max **32** electrons.

⇨ **The last shell, called the *valence shell*, can never hold more than 8 electrons**. (With the exception of **H** (#1) and **He** (#2). These elements can only hold **2** electrons in their last shell, since their last shell is also shell 1.) The electrons in the last shell are called ***valence electrons***.

➜ The electron configuration of C in the **KEY** is **2-4**. This means that the first shell, closest to the nucleus, contains 2 electrons, while the second shell contains 4 electrons. We see that carbon contains a total of 6 electrons, which makes sense, since its atomic number is 6.

➜ The electron configuration of **K** (#19) is **2-8-8-1**. Although the third shell can normally hold up to 18 electrons, it only has 8, since the last shell can't hold more than 8 electrons.

➔ *Ground vs· Excited States:*

⇨ **Ground state** → As stated above, electrons generally fill up available shells beginning from the nucleus and then moving outwards, using the least energy possible. This configuration is called ground state.

⇨ **Excited state** → Sometimes, though, if an atom gets more energy through heat or electricity, one or more of its electrons will "jump" to a higher energy level – a further out shell, before filling previous shells.

✓ <u>Ex:</u> Instead of a configuration of **2-1**, it will have a configuration of **1-2**, because one of the electrons from the first shell jumped to the second shell.

✓ <u>Ex:</u> 2-**7-1** instead of 2-**8**

⇨ One can tell whether a given configuration is in ground or excited state by *comparing it to the configuration of that element on the PT*. On the PT, the configuration is always in ground state.

➔ <u>Example 1:</u> Which electron configuration represents a potassium atom in an excited state? (1) 2-7-6 (2) 2-8-5 (3) 2-8-8-1 (4) 2-8-7-2

⇨ Look at potassium's electron configuration on the PT (#19). It is 2-8-8-1, totaling 19 electrons.

⇨ This is potassium's electron configuration in *ground* state, so choice 3 can't be the correct one.

⇨ The correct choice must add up to 19 electrons because when an atom gets to an excited state, it doesn't lose electrons – it simply rearranges them.

⇨ **Choice 4** is the only choice that has 19 electrons. (And notice that the third shell only has 7 electrons instead of 8, while the last shell has 2 electrons instead of 1.)

➔ <u>Example 2:</u> Which electron configuration represents the electrons of an atom in an excited state? (1) 2-1 (2) 2-7-4 (3) 2-8-7 (4) 2-4

⇨ This time, the name of an element is not mentioned, so you cannot compare the choices to the PT.

⇨ Look for the choice that has a shell not full to its capacity (2 in shell 1, 8 in shell 2...) yet has begun to add electrons into a further shell.

⇨ **Choice 2** has only 7 electrons in the second shell instead of 8 and yet already has electrons in the third shell. This must be the correct choice.

♦ The small number(s) on the *upper right* are **selected oxidation states**, or possible charges when the atom becomes an ion.

➔ An atom on its own is **neutral** (has no charge), since it has an *equal number of protons (+ charge) and electrons (- charge).*

➔ However, when atoms bond with other atoms in an ionic bond, they will either transfer one or more of their electrons to the other atom and become a *positively* charged **ion** (because they now have more protons than electrons) or accept those electrons and become a *negatively* charged **ion** (because they now have more electrons than protons).

➔ Atoms bond to become **stable** → have a full valence shell of 8 electrons.

➔ Selected oxidation states are the typical charge(s) of each element when it is ionically bonded. If there is more than one charge, as there is in the **KEY**, use the uppermost one when dealing with binary compounds (2 different elements in a formula).

➔ Oxidation states are used when writing **chemical formulas**, such as the formula for **lithium oxide**.
  ⇨ To write its formula, **follow these steps**:
    ✓ Write out the **symbols** of each element with their oxidation states: $Li^{+1}O^{+2}$
    ✓ **"Crisscross"** each charge, changing it to a subscript of the other element. Omit the charge: Li_2O_1
    ✓ If any of the subscripts is a 1, leave it out (because the 1 is understood): Li_2O
    ✓ If one subscript is a factor of the other (not applicable here), **simplify**. Mg_2S_2 would become MgS.
  ⇨ If a transition element (from Groups 3-12) has *multiple oxidation states*, the charge to be used will be indicated using **Roman numerals in parenthesis** after the element's name. Otherwise, just use the uppermost charge. <u>Ex:</u> For the formula of **lead (IV) oxide**:
    ✓ Write the element's symbol with its charge: $Pb^{+4}O^{-2}$
    ✓ "Crisscross:" Pb_2O_4
    ✓ Simplify: PbO_2

1. In the ground state, an atom of which element has seven valence electrons?
   (1) sodium   (3) nitrogen
   (2) phosphorus   (4) fluorine

2. Which electron configuration represents an atom of chlorine in an excited state?
   (1) 2-8-7-2 (2) 2-8-7 (3) 2-8-8 (4) 2-7-8

3. Which electron configuration represents the electrons of an atom in an excited state?
   (1) 2–2 (2) 2–2–1 (3) 2–8 (4) 2–8–1

4. Which electron configuration represents the electrons in an atom of sodium in the ground state at STP?
   (1) 2-8-1 (2) 2-7-2 (3) 2-8-6 (4) 2-7-7

5. *The weighted average of the atomic masses of the naturally occurring isotopes of an element is the
   (1) atomic mass of the element
   (2) atomic number of the element
   (3) mass number of each isotope
   (4) formula mass of each isotope

6. What is the formula for iron(II) oxide?
   (1) FeO (2) FeO_2 (3) Fe_2O (4) Fe_2O_3

7. What is the total number of neutrons in an atom of K-42?
   (1) 19   (2) 20   (3) 23   (4) 42

8. Some isotopes of neon are Ne-19, Ne-20, Ne-21, Ne-22, and Ne-24. The neon-24 decays by beta emission. The atomic mass and natural abundance for the naturally occurring isotopes of neon are shown in the table to the right. State the number of neutrons in an atom of Ne-20 and the number of neutrons in an atom of Ne-22.

Naturally Occurring Isotopes of Neon

Isotope Notation	Atomic Mass (u)	Natural Abundance (%)
Ne-20	19.99	90.48
Ne-21	20.99	0.27
Ne-22	21.99	9.25

Questions 9 & 10: The table below shows data for three isotopes of the same element.

9. State the number of valence electrons in an atom of isotope D in the ground state.

10. *Compare the energy of an electron in the first electron shell to the energy of an electron in the second electron shell in an atom of isotope E.

Data for Three Isotopes of an Element

Isotopes	Number of Protons	Number of Neutrons	Atomic Mass (u)	Natural Abundance (%)
Atom D	12	12	23.99	78.99
Atom E	12	13	24.99	10.00
Atom G	12	14	25.98	11.01

Reading the Table (Part II):

♦ Elements are arranged in order of ***increasing atomic number***. Table S is also arranged this way.

♦ The table is divided into *rows* and *columns*:

➔ ***Period*** → *horizontal* row on the **PT**.

⇨ Periods have elements with the *same number of occupied shells*.

➔ ***Group*** → *vertical* column on the **PT**.

⇨ Groups have elements with the same number of *valence electrons* (1, 2, 13-18 – "representative groups" → rule doesn't apply to groups 3-12).

⇨ The number of valence electrons very much affects the *chemical properties* of an element. Therefore, elements within a group have similar properties.

♦ <u>Trends on the Periodic Table:</u>

➔ The following are common trends, or patterns, found on the **PT**. While it isn't necessary to memorize the trends, since they can easily be figured out using **Table S** (as explained below), it may be helpful to familiarize yourself with them to save time on the regents.

⇨ ***First ionization energy*** decreases going down a **group** and *increases* going across a **period** (l→r).

✓ **First ionization energy** - the amount of energy required to remove one of an atom's valence (most loosely bound) electrons. The *more difficult* it is to *remove* the atom's valence electrons, the *higher* its first ionization energy (FIE).

⇨ ***Electronegativity*** follows the **same trend** as first ionization energy.

✓ **Electronegativity** – the strength of the attraction an atom has for the electrons in a chemical bond. The *stronger* the atom's *attraction* for another atom's valence electrons during bonding, the *higher* its electronegativity.

✓ An exception to this rule is **Group 18**, which has high FIE but no electronegativity value at all. This is because Group 18 atoms have complete valence shells and therefore are already stable, so it is extremely difficult to remove its valence electrons (= high FIE); however it has no attraction to another atom's electrons since it isn't "looking" to become stable through bonding.

⇨ **Atomic/ionic radius** *increases* going down a **group** and *decreases* going across a **period**.

  ✓ **Atomic/ionic radius** – the approximate radius (distance from the nucleus to the outer "boundaries") of the atom or ion (Atoms aren't surrounded by a rigid wall – that's why it is only approximate.)

➔ You can use **Table S** to look up the above trends as follows:

⇨ Look up each element in the referenced group/row on **Table S**, using its atomic number. When referencing a group (as opposed to a row), it may be helpful to write down each number before you look at **Table S**, so you don't need to keep flipping back and forth between the **PT** and **Table S**. (Rows are consecutive numbers, while groups are not.)

⇨ Check either the **FIRST IONIZATION ENERGY** column, the **ELECTRONEGATIVITY** column or the **ATOMIC RADIUS** column, depending on what the question is asking. Write down the values of each element referenced.

⇨ Determine whether the F.I.E./electronegativity/atomic radius is *increasing* or *decreasing*, based on the values you looked up.

➔ Example 1:

⇨ Which general trends in first ionization energy and electronegativity values are demonstrated by Group 15 elements as they are considered in order from top to bottom?

  (1) The first ionization energy decreases and the electronegativity decreases.
  (2) The first ionization energy increases and the electronegativity increases.
  (3) The first ionization energy decreases and the electronegativity increases.
  (4) The first ionization energy increases and the electronegativity decreases.

  ✓ Look up Group 15 elements' atomic numbers, and list them in order from t→b: **7, 15, 33, 51, 83** (leave out 115 because **Table S** only goes until 89).

  ✓ Since you (might) know that first ionization energy and electronegativity follow *the same trend*, only look up one of them. The first ionization energy values for the above elements, in that order, are **1402, 1012, 944, 831, 703**.

  ✓ Clearly, first ionization energy decreases as you go down a group. **Choice 1** is the correct choice.

➜ Example 2:

⇨ Which general trend is found in Period 3 as the elements are considered in order of increasing atomic number?

(1) increasing atomic radius   (3) decreasing atomic mass

(2) increasing electronegativity   (4) decreasing first ionization energy

✓ Look up Period 3 elements' atomic numbers: **11, 12, 13... 18**. (Notice that here it isn't necessary to write down the list, since they are consecutive numbers and easy to remember.)

✓ On **Table S**, check each choice and figure out whether it is true.

✓ **Choice 2** is the correct choice. Electronegativity increases going across a period from l→r.

Understanding the Trends

First Ionization Energy:

An atom has higher first ionization energy (FIE), making it more difficult to remove its valence electrons, when...

➜ It has **fewer shells** → because its valence electrons are relatively close to the positively charged nucleus and therefore have a stronger attraction to it

⇨ When going *down a group*, FIE will **decrease** because as the number of shells increases, it gets easier and easier to remove a valence electron.

➜ It has **more protons** (when has same number of shells but more protons) → because there is a stronger pull on the electrons, securing them in place better

⇨ When going *across a period*, FIE will **increase** because as the number of protons increases, it gets more and more difficult to remove an electron.

Electronegativity:

Electronegativity follows the same trend as F.I.E. because when little energy is required (it is easy) to remove an atom's own electrons (= low F.I.E.), it will certainly not be able to take away another atom's electrons easily → it will have a low attraction to those electrons → low electronegativity.

Atomic Radius:

➜ Atomic radius **increases** when going *down a group* because when an atom has **more shells**, its atomic radius will be larger (and if **fewer shells** – smaller atomic radius).

➜ Atomic radius **decreases** when going *across a period* because the **more protons** there are (within the same number of shells), the stronger the electrons' attraction to the nucleus.

Reading the Table (Part III)

♦ The elements on the **PT** are classified into four categories: **metals**, **nonmetals**, **metalloids** and **noble gases**. Taking each category one by one:

➔ *Metals* → found to the *left* of the "steps" (the dark black zigzag dividing line on the right of the table).

⇨ The Metals on the <u>PT</u>:

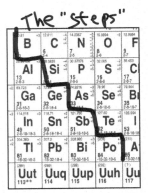

✓ **All elements** in Group 1 *besides H (hydrogen)*

✓ **All elements** within Groups 2-12

✓ **All elements** *besides B (boron)* in Group 13

✓ **Sn** (tin) **and down** in Group 14

✓ **Bi** (bismuth) **and down** in Group 15

✓ **Po** (polonium) **and down** in Group 16

⇨ Metals have *few valence electrons*, which causes them to **lose** their valence electrons and form **positive** ions when ionically bonding.

✓ <u>Ex 1:</u> **Na**, with an electron configuration of (2-8-**1**), would *lose* its single valence electron while bonding to have a full valence shell of eight. Its new electron configuration would be (2-8). This would cause it to have one more positively charged proton than negatively charged electrons, which gives it its oxidation state of **+1**.

✓ <u>Ex 2:</u> **Ca**, with an electron configuration of (2-8-8-**2**), would lose its two valence electrons while bonding and now have a configuration of (2-8-8) with an oxidation state of **+2**.

⇨ Some **physical properties** of metals:

✓ Malleable and ductile – can be pounded into sheets and made into wires

✓ Good conductors of heat and electricity

✓ Luster – a shine

"A metaL Loses. If there's a gaiN, Non-metal."

➔ **Nonmetals** → found to the *right* of the "steps."

⇨ The Nonmetals on the <u>PT</u>:

- ✓ **C** (carbon) in Group 14

- ✓ **N** (nitrogen) and **P** (phosphorus) in Group 15

- ✓ **O** (oxygen) **through Se** (selenium) in Group 16

- ✓ **F** (fluorine) **and down** in Group 17

⇨ Nonmetals have *many valence electrons*, which causes them to **gain** electrons and form **negative** ions when ionically bonding.

- ✓ <u>Ex 1:</u> **O**, with an electron configuration of (2-**6**), would *gain* two valence electron while bonding to have a full valence shell of eight. Its new electron configuration would be (2-8). This would cause it to have two more negatively charged electrons than positively charged protons, which gives it its oxidation state of -**2**.

- ✓ <u>Ex 2:</u> **I**, with an electron configuration of (2-8-18-18-**7**), would *gain* one valence electrons while bonding and now have a configuration of (2-8-18-18-**8**) with an oxidation state of -**1**.

⇨ Some **physical properties** of nonmetals:

- ✓ Brittle – break into pieces easily – not malleable or ductile

- ✓ Poor conductors of heat and electricity

- ✓ No luster

➔ **Metalloids** → found *touching* the "steps." The tricky thing is that only six of the nine elements touching the "steps" are metalloids. It would be a good idea to memorize the six metalloids by reciting the mnemonic in the sidebar while looking at the PT to see what each word stands for.

Big Silly Gerls Ask Sarabenson [if they could use her] Telephone

⇨ Metalloids have some chemical properties of **metals** and some of **nonmetals**.

⇨ Metalloids on the <u>PT</u>:

- ✓ **B** (boron)
- ✓ **Si** (silicon)
- ✓ **Ge** (germanium)

- ✓ **As** (arsenic)
- ✓ **Sb** (antinomy)
- ✓ **Te** (tellurium)

→ *Noble Gases* → Group 18, on the far right of the table

⇨ Noble gases have **full valence shells**, which causes them to *rarely bond* with other elements. (They are too "noble" to mix with common folk!)

⇨ Noble Gases on the **PT**:

   ✓ **All elements** in Group 18, including **He** (helium), floating slightly above the rest of the group.

> All noble gases end in "on" besides He (helium):
> - Neon
> - Argon
> - Krypton
> - Xenon
> - Radon

♦ Elements in all three **states of matter** are found on the **PT**. While it isn't necessary to memorize the states of matter, since they can be figured out using **Table S** (as explained in the next section), memorizing them will save you time on the regents.

→ *Solids* on the **PT** include:

⇨ **All elements** not specified below

→ *Liquids* on the **PT** include:

⇨ **Hg** (mercury) in Group 12

⇨ **Br** (bromine) in Group 17

→ *Gases* on the **PT** include:

⇨ **H** (hydrogen) in Group 1

⇨ **N** (nitrogen) and **P** (phosphorus) in Group 15

⇨ **O** (oxygen) in Group 16

⇨ **F** (fluorine) and **Cl** (chlorine) in Group 17

⇨ **All elements in Group 18** (The "Noble Gases"), including **He** (helium) floating slightly above the rest of the group

14. As the first five elements in Group 14 are considered in order from top to bottom, there are changes in both the
    (1) number of valence shell electrons and number of first shell electrons
    (2) electronegativity values and number of first shell electrons
    (3) number of valence shell electrons and atomic radii
    (4) electronegativity values and atomic radii

15. *Which element is classified as a metalloid?
    (1) Te (2) S (3) Hg (4) I

16. *Which element is malleable at STP?
    (1) Chlorine   (3) helium
    (2) Copper   (4) sulfur

17. The elements on the Periodic Table of the Elements are arranged in order of increasing
    (1) atomic mass   (3) atomic number
    (2) formula mass (4) oxidation number

18. As the elements in Period 2 of the Periodic Table are considered in order from left to right, which property generally decreases?
    (1) atomic radius   (3) ionization energy
    (2) electronegativity (4) nuclear charge

19. *Which electrons in a calcium atom in the ground state have the greatest effect on the chemical properties of calcium?
    (1) the two electrons in the 1st shell
    (2) the two electrons in the 4th shell
    (3) the eight electrons in the 2nd shell
    (4) the eight electrons in the 3rd shell

20. Which group on the Periodic Table has two elements that exist as gases at STP?
    (1) 1 (2) 2 (3) 16 (4) 17

21. Which element tends not to react with other elements?
    (1) Helium   (3) phosphorus
    (2) Hydrogen   (4) potassium

22. Based on Table S, which group on the Periodic Table has the element with the highest electronegativity?
    (1) 1 (2) 2 (3) 17 (4) 18

23. Which ion in the ground state has the same electron configuration as an atom of neon in the ground state?
    (1) Ca^{2+} (2) Cl^- (3) Li^+ (4) O^{2-}

24. In which group on the Periodic Table would a nonmetallic element belong if atoms of this element tend to gain two electrons to complete their valence shell?
    (1) 14   (2) 15 (3) 16 (4) 17

25. *Which list represents the classification of the elements nitrogen, neon, magnesium, and silicon, respectively?
    (1) metal, metalloid, nonmetal, noble gas
    (2) nonmetal, noble gas, metal, metalloid
    (3) nonmetal, metalloid, noble gas, metal
    (4) noble gas, metal, metalloid, nonmetal

26. In the ground state, all atoms of Group 15 elements have the same number of
    (1) valence electrons (3) neutrons
    (2) electron shells   (4) protons

27. *Which term represents the strength of the attraction an atom has for the electrons in a chemical bond?
    (1) electrical conductivity
    (2) electronegativity

(3) first ionization energy

(4) specific heat capacity

28. Which trend is observed as the first four elements in Group 17 on the Periodic Table are considered in order of increasing atomic number?

(1) Electronegativity increases.

(2) First ionization energy decreases.

(3) The number of valence electrons increases.

(4) The number of electron shells decreases.

29. The arrangement of the elements from left to right in Period 4 on the Periodic Table is based on

(1) atomic mass

(2) atomic number

(3) the number of electron shells

(4) the number of oxidation states

30. Magnesium and calcium have similar chemical properties because their atoms in the ground state have

(1) equal numbers of protons and electrons

(2) equal numbers of protons and neutrons

(3) two electrons in the first shell

(4) two electrons in the outermost shell

Questions 31-33: *The elements in Group 2 on the Periodic Table can be compared in terms of first ionization energy, electronegativity, and other general properties.*

31. Describe the general trend in electronegativity as the metals in Group 2 on the Periodic Table are considered in order of increasing atomic number.

32. Explain, in terms of atomic structure, why barium has a lower first ionization energy than magnesium.

33. State the general trend in first ionization energy as the elements in Period 3 are considered from left to right.

Questions 34-36: *Periodic trends are observed in the properties of the elements in Period 3 on the Periodic Table. These elements vary in physical properties, such as phase, and in chemical properties, such as their ability to lose or gain electrons during a chemical reaction.*

34. Identify the metals in Period 3 on the Periodic Table.

35. Identify the element in Period 3 that requires the least amount of energy to remove the most loosely held electrons from a mole of gaseous atoms of the element in the ground state.

36. State the general trend in atomic radius as the elements in Period 3 are considered in order of increasing atomic number.

37. Compare the atomic radius of an atom of iodine to the atomic radius of an atom of rubidium when both atoms are in the ground state.

38. Identify the noble gas that has atoms with the same electron configuration as the metal ions in rubidium chloride, when both the atoms and the ions are in the ground state.

NEW YORK STATE
CHEMISTRY REFERENCE TABLES

TABLE S

PROPERTIES OF SELECTED ELEMENTS

Table S
Properties of Selected Elements

Atomic Number	Symbol	Name	First Ionization Energy (kJ/mol)	Electronegativity	Melting Point (K)	Boiling Point (K)	Density** (g/cm³)	Atomic Radius (pm)
1	H	hydrogen	1312	2.2	14	20	0.000082	32
2	He	helium	2372	—	—	4	0.000164	37
3	Li	lithium	520	1.0	454	1615	0.534	130
4	Be	beryllium	900	1.6	1560	2744	1.85	99
5	B	boron	801	2.0	2348	4273	2.34	84
6	C	carbon	1086	2.6	—	—	—	75
7	N	nitrogen	1402	3.0	63	77	0.001145	71
8	O	oxygen	1314	3.4	54	90	0.001308	64
9	F	fluorine	1681	4.0	53	85	0.001553	60
10	Ne	neon	2081	—	24	27	0.000825	62
11	Na	sodium	496	0.9	371	1156	0.97	160
12	Mg	magnesium	738	1.3	923	1363	1.74	140
13	Al	aluminum	578	1.6	933	2792	2.70	124
14	Si	silicon	787	1.9	1687	3538	2.3296	114
15	P	phosphorus (white)	1012	2.2	317	554	1.823	109
16	S	sulfur (monoclinic)	1000	2.6	388	718	2.00	104
17	Cl	chlorine	1251	3.2	172	239	0.002898	100
18	Ar	argon	1521	—	84	87	0.001633	101
19	K	potassium	419	0.8	337	1032	0.89	200
20	Ca	calcium	590	1.0	1115	1757	1.54	174
21	Sc	scandium	633	1.4	1814	3109	2.99	159
22	Ti	titanium	659	1.5	1941	3560	4.506	148
23	V	vanadium	651	1.6	2183	3680	6.0	144
24	Cr	chromium	653	1.7	2180	2944	7.15	130
25	Mn	manganese	717	1.6	1519	2334	7.3	129
26	Fe	iron	762	1.8	1811	3134	7.87	124
27	Co	cobalt	760	1.9	1768	3200	8.86	118
28	Ni	nickel	737	1.9	1728	3186	8.90	117
29	Cu	copper	745	1.9	1358	2835	8.96	122
30	Zn	zinc	906	1.7	693	1180	7.134	120
31	Ga	gallium	579	1.8	303	2477	5.91	123
32	Ge	germanium	762	2.0	1211	3106	5.3234	120
33	As	arsenic (gray)	944	2.2	1090	—	5.75	120
34	Se	selenium (gray)	941	2.6	494	958	4.809	118
35	Br	bromine	1140	3.0	266	332	3.1028	117
36	Kr	krypton	1351	—	116	120	0.003425	116
37	Rb	rubidium	403	0.8	312	961	1.53	215
38	Sr	strontium	549	1.0	1050	1655	2.64	190
39	Y	yttrium	600	1.2	1795	3618	4.47	176
40	Zr	zirconium	640	1.3	2128	4682	6.52	164

Atomic Number	Symbol	Name	First Ionization Energy (kJ/mol)	Electronegativity	Melting Point (K)	Boiling Point (K)	Density** (g/cm³)	Atomic Radius (pm)
41	Nb	niobium	652	1.6	2750	5017	8.57	156
42	Mo	molybdenum	684	2.2	2896	4912	10.2	146
43	Tc	technetium	702	2.1	2430	4538	11	138
44	Ru	ruthenium	710	2.2	2606	4423	12.1	136
45	Rh	rhodium	720	2.3	2237	3968	12.4	134
46	Pd	palladium	804	2.2	1828	3236	12.0	130
47	Ag	silver	731	1.9	1235	2435	10.5	136
48	Cd	cadmium	868	1.7	594	1040	8.69	140
49	In	indium	558	1.8	430	2345	7.31	142
50	Sn	tin (white)	709	2.0	505	2875	7.287	140
51	Sb	antimony (gray)	831	2.1	904	1860	6.68	140
52	Te	tellurium	869	2.1	723	1261	6.232	137
53	I	iodine	1008	2.7	387	457	4.933	136
54	Xe	xenon	1170	2.6	161	165	0.005366	136
55	Cs	cesium	376	0.8	302	944	1.873	238
56	Ba	barium	503	0.9	1000	2170	3.62	206
57	La	lanthanum	538	1.1	1193	3737	6.15	194

Elements 58–71 have been omitted.

Atomic Number	Symbol	Name	First Ionization Energy (kJ/mol)	Electronegativity	Melting Point (K)	Boiling Point (K)	Density** (g/cm³)	Atomic Radius (pm)
72	Hf	hafnium	659	1.3	2506	4876	13.3	164
73	Ta	tantalum	728	1.5	3290	5731	16.4	158
74	W	tungsten	759	1.7	3695	5828	19.3	150
75	Re	rhenium	756	1.9	3458	5869	20.8	141
76	Os	osmium	814	2.2	3306	5285	22.587	136
77	Ir	iridium	865	2.2	2719	4701	22.562	132
78	Pt	platinum	864	2.2	2041	4098	21.5	130
79	Au	gold	890	2.4	1337	3129	19.3	130
80	Hg	mercury	1007	1.9	234	630	13.5336	132
81	Tl	thallium	589	1.8	577	1746	11.8	144
82	Pb	lead	716	1.8	600	2022	11.3	145
83	Bi	bismuth	703	1.9	544	1837	9.79	150
84	Po	polonium	812	2.0	527	1235	9.20	142
85	At	astatine	—	2.2	575	—	—	148
86	Rn	radon	1037	—	202	211	0.009074	146
87	Fr	francium	393	0.7	300	—	—	242
88	Ra	radium	509	0.9	969	—	5	211
89	Ac	actinium	499	1.1	1323	3471	10.	201

Elements 90 and above have been omitted.

* boiling point at standard pressure
** density of solids and liquids at room temperature and density of gases at 298 K and 101.3 kPa
— no data available
Source: CRC Handbook for Chemistry and Physics, 91st ed. 2010–2011, CRC Press

TABLE S: Properties of Selected Elements

Table S
Properties of Selected Elements

Atomic Number	Symbol	Name	First Ionization Energy (kJ/mol)	Electro-negativity	Melting Point (K)	Boiling* Point (K)	Density** (g/cm³)	Atomic Radius (pm)
1	H	hydrogen	1312	2.2	14	20.	0.000082	32
2	He	helium	2372	—	—	4	0.000164	37
3	Li	lithium	520.	1.0	454	1615	0.534	130.
4	Be	beryllium	900.	1.6	1560.	2744	1.85	99
5	B	boron	801	2.0	2348	4273	2.34	84
6	C	carbon	1086	2.6	—	—	—	75
7	N	nitrogen	1402	3.0	63	77	0.001145	71
8	O	oxygen	1314	3.4	54	90.	0.001308	64
9	F	fluorine	1681	4.0	53	85	0.001553	60.
10	Ne	neon	2081	—	24	27	0.000825	62
11	Na	sodium	496	0.9	371	1156	0.97	160.
12	Mg	magnesium	738	1.3	923	1363	1.74	140.
13	Al	aluminum	578	1.6	933	2792	2.70	124
14	Si	silicon	787	1.9	1687	3538	2.3296	114
15	P	phosphorus (white)	1012	2.2	317	554	1.823	109
16	S	sulfur (monoclinic)	1000.	2.6	388	718	2.00	104
17	Cl	chlorine	1251	3.2	172	239	0.002898	100.
18	Ar	argon	1521	—	84	87	0.001633	101
19	K	potassium	419	0.8	337	1032	0.89	200.
20	Ca	calcium	590.	1.0	1115	1757	1.54	174
21	Sc	scandium	633	1.4	1814	3109	2.99	159
22	Ti	titanium	659	1.5	1941	3560.	4.506	148
23	V	vanadium	651	1.6	2183	3680.	6.0	144
24	Cr	chromium	653	1.7	2180.	2944	7.15	130.
25	Mn	manganese	717	1.6	1519	2334	7.3	129
26	Fe	iron	762	1.8	1811	3134	7.87	124
27	Co	cobalt	760.	1.9	1768	3200.	8.86	118
28	Ni	nickel	737	1.9	1728	3186	8.90	117
29	Cu	copper	745	1.9	1358	2835	8.96	122
30	Zn	zinc	906	1.7	693	1180.	7.134	120.
31	Ga	gallium	579	1.8	303	2477	5.91	123
32	Ge	germanium	762	2.0	1211	3106	5.3234	120.
33	As	arsenic (gray)	944	2.2	1090.	—	5.75	120.
34	Se	selenium (gray)	941	2.6	494	958	4.809	118
35	Br	bromine	1140.	3.0	266	332	3.1028	117
36	Kr	krypton	1351	—	116	120.	0.003425	116
37	Rb	rubidium	403	0.8	312	961	1.53	215
38	Sr	strontium	549	1.0	1050.	1655	2.64	190.
39	Y	yttrium	600.	1.2	1795	3618	4.47	176
40	Zr	zirconium	640.	1.3	2128	4682	6.52	164

Atomic Number	Symbol	Name	First Ionization Energy (kJ/mol)	Electro-negativity	Melting Point (K)	Boiling* Point (K)	Density** (g/cm³)	Atomic Radius (pm)
41	Nb	niobium	652	1.6	2750.	5017	8.57	156
42	Mo	molybdenum	684	2.2	2896	4912	10.2	146
43	Tc	technetium	702	2.1	2430.	4538	11	138
44	Ru	ruthenium	710.	2.2	2606	4423	12.1	136
45	Rh	rhodium	720.	2.3	2237	3968	12.4	134
46	Pd	palladium	804	2.2	1828	3236	12.0	130.
47	Ag	silver	731	1.9	1235	2435	10.5	136
48	Cd	cadmium	868	1.7	594	1040.	8.69	140.
49	In	indium	558	1.8	430.	2345	7.31	142
50	Sn	tin (white)	709	2.0	505	2875	7.287	140.
51	Sb	antimony (gray)	831	2.1	904	1860.	6.68	140.
52	Te	tellurium	869	2.1	723	1261	6.232	137
53	I	iodine	1008	2.7	387	457	4.933	136
54	Xe	xenon	1170.	2.6	161	165	0.005366	136
55	Cs	cesium	376	0.8	302	944	1.873	238
56	Ba	barium	503	0.9	1000.	2170.	3.62	206
57	La	lanthanum	538	1.1	1193	3737	6.15	194
Elements 58–71 have been omitted.								
72	Hf	hafnium	659	1.3	2506	4876	13.3	164
73	Ta	tantalum	728	1.5	3290.	5731	16.4	158
74	W	tungsten	759	1.7	3695	5828	19.3	150.
75	Re	rhenium	756	1.9	3458	5869	20.8	141
76	Os	osmium	814	2.2	3306	5285	22.587	136
77	Ir	iridium	865	2.2	2719	4701	22.562	132
78	Pt	platinum	864	2.2	2041	4098	21.5	130.
79	Au	gold	890.	2.4	1337	3129	19.3	130.
80	Hg	mercury	1007	1.9	234	630.	13.5336	132
81	Tl	thallium	589	1.8	577	1746	11.8	144
82	Pb	lead	716	1.8	600.	2022	11.3	145
83	Bi	bismuth	703	1.9	544	1837	9.79	150.
84	Po	polonium	812	2.0	527	1235	9.20	142
85	At	astatine	—	2.2	575	—	—	148
86	Rn	radon	1037	—	202	211	0.009074	146
87	Fr	francium	393	0.7	300.	—	—	242
88	Ra	radium	509	0.9	969	—	5	211
89	Ac	actinium	499	1.1	1323	3471	10.	201
Elements 90 and above have been omitted.								

*boiling point at standard pressure
**density of solids and liquids at room temperature and density of gases at 298 K and 101.3 kPa
— no data available
Source: *CRC Handbook for Chemistry and Physics*, 91st ed., 2010–2011, CRC Press

Reading the Table:

♦ Table S, like the **PT**, is organized according to each elements' **ATOMIC NUMBER** (the first column on the left), which is followed by its **SYMBOL** and **NAME**, already discussed in the previous section.

Table S, as stated in the previous section, supplements the Periodic Table by providing additional information about some of the elements (**1-57** and **72-89**). Much of this table has already been discussed in the previous section, **The Periodic Table of the Elements**.

→ Use the **NAME** column to answer questions asking you to determine whether a specific substance is an element or a compound (two or more elements combined). Such questions are usually phrased as follows:

⇨ "Which substance *can* be broken down by chemical means / a chemical change?"

✓ This question is asking you which substance is *not* an element, since elements cannot be broken down by chemical means.

⇨ "Which substance *cannot* be broken...?"

✓ This question is asking you which substance *is* an element.

→ If the substance's name is listed in this column, it is an element, since the PT and Table S only contain pure elements. Otherwise, it is a compound. (Although Table S does not include all elements on the PT, any regents questions of this type will not include elements not on Table S.)

♦ The next column, **FIRST IONIZATION ENERGY**, was also already discussed in the previous section.

♦ The **ELECTRONEGATIVITY** column was partially discussed, but there is still one very important point to mention: This column is often used when determining whether a chemical bond is covalent or ionic.

→ To figure out the type of bond within a given compound:

⇨ Look up their electronegativities on Table S.

⇨ Subtract them (smaller number from larger number).

✓ If the difference is less than or equal to (≤) 1.7, the bond is *covalent*.

✓ If the difference is greater than 1.7, the bond is *ionic*.

✓ The greater the difference between the two electronegativities, the more **polar** the bond.

♦ The **MELTING POINT** and **BOILING POINT** columns give you the temperature in Kelvins at which each element will melt/freeze and boil/condense, depending on whether it is gaining or losing energy.

→ Note the asterisk* after the word "Boiling" on the table. This indicates that the boiling point given is at **standard pressure**. If the outside pressure were higher, the boiling point would be higher and vice versa. (See Table H: Vapor Pressure of Four Liquids for a more detailed discussion on boiling points.)

➔ As referenced in the previous section, by using an element's melting point and boiling point and the following steps, one can figure out its state of matter at *STP* (see **Table A: Standard Temperature and Pressure**) or at any other given temperature:

⇨ Draw a quick number line with the element's melting point plotted on the left and boiling point plotted on the right.

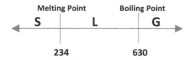

✓ Put an "S" for "solid" to the left of the melting point, since if the element's current temperature is lower than its melting point – it hasn't gotten warm enough to melt yet, it will be in a solid state.

✓ Put an "L" for "liquid" between the melting point and boiling point, since if the element's temperature is between its melting point and boiling point – it was warm enough to melt but not warm enough to evaporate, it is in a liquid state.

✓ Put a "G" for "gas" to the right of the boiling point, since if the element's temperature is above its boiling point – it already evaporated, it will be a gas.

⇨ Plot the temperature you're given. Based on where it falls on your number line, determine its state of matter.

➔ <u>Example 1:</u> In what state of matter is mercury at STP?

⇨ Look up mercury (atomic #80) on **Table S**. Its melting point is **234 K** and boiling point is **630 K**. Plot these values on a number line.

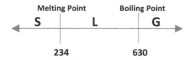

⇨ As seen on **Table A: Standard Temperature and Pressure**, standard temperature in Kelvins is **273**. Plot it on your number line.

⇨ At STP, the temperature of mercury falls between its melting point and boiling point. It is therefore a **liquid.**

➔ **Example 2:** In what state of matter is sodium at 1159 K?

⇨ Look up sodium (atomic #11) on **Table S**. Its melting point is **371 K** and boiling point is **1156 K**. Plot these values on a number line.

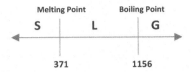

⇨ Plot the given temperature, 1159 K, on your number line.

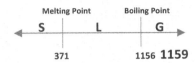

⇨ At 1159 K, the temperature of sodium is above its boiling point. It is therefore a **gas.**

➔ When given a list of elements and asked to choose the solid/liquid/gas among them at a specific temperature:

⇨ For **solids**: determine which element's **melting point** is *above* the given temperature. This would mean it has not yet reached its melting point and thus is a solid.

✓ Which element is a solid at 590° K?

    a. Thallium   c. Bismuth
    b. Lead   d. Polonium

⇨ For **liquids**: determine which element's **melting point** falls *below* the given temperature and **boiling point** falls *above* it.

✓ Which element is a liquid at 600° K?

    a. Silver   c. Iodine
    b. Cadmium   d. Bromine

⇨ For **gases**: determine which element's **boiling point** is *below* the given temperature. This would mean it has already reached its boiling point and thus is a gas.

✓ Which element is a gas at 600° K?

    a. Lithium   c. Phosphorus
    b. Sodium   d. Iron

- ◆ The **DENSITY** column is very straightforward. It simply states the density, in grams per cubic centimeter (g/cm³), of each element at STP. This column is used most often together with the **percent of error** equation on **Table T: Important Formulas and Equations.** You are given a student's erroneous calculation of an element's density and then asked to calculate the percent of error. To do this, look up the correct measurement for that element's density – on **Table S.**

- ◆ The **ATOMIC RADIUS** column was previously discussed in the last section. An additional point, however, is when asked to compare **ionic radii**, between two ions of the same type (both positive or both negative), use this column, since the trend would be the same. Meaning, if Element X's *atomic* radius is larger than Element Y's atomic radius, Element X's *ionic* radius would also be larger than Element Y's ionic radius.

---

1. Which substance cannot be broken down by a chemical change?
   (1) Ammonia
   (2) tungsten
   (3) ethanol
   (4) water

2. Which substance can be broken down by chemical means?
   (1) Ammonia
   (2) Aluminum
   (3) antimony
   (4) argon

3. At 298 K and 1 atm, which noble gas has the lowest density?
   (1) Ne (2) Kr (3) Xe (4) R

4. Which element is a liquid at 1000. K?
   (1) Ag (2) Al (3) Ca (4) Ni

5. The least polar bond is found in a molecule of
   (1) HI (2) HF (3) HCl (4) HBr

6. Which ion has the largest radius?
   (1) Br^-
   (2) Cl^-
   (3) F^-
   (4) I^-

7. Which group on the Periodic Table has at least one element in each of the three phases of matter at STP?
   (1) 1 (2) 2 (3) 17 (4) 18

8. *The degree of polarity of a covalent bond between two atoms is determined by calculating the difference in their
   (1) atomic radii
   (2) melting points
   (3) electronegativities
   (4) ionization energies

9. Based on Table S, an atom of which element has the strongest attraction for electrons in a chemical bond?
   (1) chlorine
   (2) nitrogen
   (3) oxygen
   (4) selenium

10. An atom of which element reacts with an atom of hydrogen to form a bond with the greatest degree of polarity?
    (1) Carbon
    (2) Fluorine
    (3) nitrogen
    (4) oxygen

11. Which element has a melting point higher than the melting point of rhenium?
    (1) iridium
    (2) osmium
    (3) tantalum
    (4) tungsten

12. Which element is a gas at STP?
    (1) sulfur   (3) potassium
    (2) xenon   (4) phosphorus

13. The formula below represents a molecule of butanamide.

$$
\begin{array}{ccccc}
H & H & H & O & H \\
| & | & | & \| & \diagup \\
H-C-C-C-C-N & & & & \\
| & | & | & & \diagdown \\
H & H & H & & H \\
\end{array}
$$

State the type of chemical bond between a hydrogen atom and the nitrogen atom in the molecule.

14. Identify the phase of chlorine at STP.

15. *In the late 1800s, Dmitri Mendeleev developed a periodic table of the elements known at that time. Based on the pattern in his periodic table, he was able to predict properties of some elements that had not yet been discovered. Information about two of these elements is shown in the table below.*

Some Element Properties Predicted by Mendeleev

Predicted Elements	Property	Predicted Value	Actual Value
eka-aluminum (Ea)	density at STP	5.9 g/cm³	5.91 g/cm³
	melting point	low	30.°C
	oxide formula	Ea_2O_3	
	approximate molar mass	68 g/mol	
eka-silicon (Es)	density at STP	5.5 g/cm³	5.3234 g/cm³
	melting point	high	938°C
	oxide formula	EsO_2	
	approximate molar mass	72 g/mol	

Identify the element that Mendeleev called eka-silicon, Es.

NEW YORK STATE
CHEMISTRY REFERENCE TABLES

TABLE T

IMPORTANT FORMULAS & EQUATIONS

Table T
Important Formulas and Equations

Density	$d = \dfrac{m}{V}$	d = density m = mass V = volume
Mole Calculations	number of moles $= \dfrac{\text{given mass}}{\text{gram-formula mass}}$	
Percent Error	% error $= \dfrac{\text{measured value} - \text{accepted value}}{\text{accepted value}} \times 100$	
Percent Composition	% composition by mass $= \dfrac{\text{mass of part}}{\text{mass of whole}} \times 100$	
Concentration	parts per million $= \dfrac{\text{mass of solute}}{\text{mass of solution}} \times 1\,000\,000$	
	molarity $= \dfrac{\text{moles of solute}}{\text{liter of solution}}$	
Combined Gas Law	$\dfrac{P_1V_1}{T_1} = \dfrac{P_2V_2}{T_2}$	P = pressure V = volume T = temperature
Titration	$M_AV_A = M_BV_B$	M_A = molarity of H^+ M_B = molarity of OH^- V_A = volume of acid V_B = volume of base
Heat	$q = mC\Delta T$ $q = mH_f$ $q = mH_v$	q = heat H_f = heat of fusion m = mass H_v = heat of vaporization C = specific heat capacity ΔT = change in temperature
Temperature	$K = {}^\circ C + 273$	K = kelvin ${}^\circ C$ = degree Celsius

TABLE T: Important Formulas & Equations

Table T
Important Formulas and Equations

Density	$d = \dfrac{m}{V}$	d = density m = mass V = volume
Mole Calculations	number of moles = $\dfrac{\text{given mass}}{\text{gram-formula mass}}$	
Percent Error	% error = $\dfrac{\text{measured value} - \text{accepted value}}{\text{accepted value}} \times 100$	
Percent Composition	% composition by mass = $\dfrac{\text{mass of part}}{\text{mass of whole}} \times 100$	
Concentration	parts per million = $\dfrac{\text{mass of solute}}{\text{mass of solution}} \times 1\,000\,000$	
	molarity = $\dfrac{\text{moles of solute}}{\text{liter of solution}}$	
Combined Gas Law	$\dfrac{P_1V_1}{T_1} = \dfrac{P_2V_2}{T_2}$	P = pressure V = volume T = temperature
Titration	$M_AV_A = M_BV_B$	M_A = molarity of H^+ M_B = molarity of OH^- V_A = volume of acid V_B = volume of base
Heat	$q = mC\Delta T$ $q = mH_f$ $q = mH_v$	q = heat H_f = heat of fusion m = mass H_v = heat of vaporization C = specific heat capacity ΔT = change in temperature
Temperature	$K = °C + 273$	K = kelvin $°C$ = degree Celsius

Table T provides 12 **mathematical formulas** (in 9 categories) used with many important chemistry concepts. Most equations are not too difficult; the trick is knowing when to use each one and being able to figure out which values to plug in where. **It is worth familiarizing yourselves with these equations.** *They come up VERY often on the chemistry regents!*

Density	$d = \frac{m}{V}$	d = density m = mass V = volume

Using the Formula:

♦ Express your answer in **correct units**, such as *grams per cubic centimeter*

♦ Besides solving for density, also be able to **solve for mass or volume** given the density and one other part of equation.

♦ <u>Example 1:</u> What is the *density* of a brick with a volume of 6 cm³ and a mass of 12 grams?

➔ Formula: $d = \frac{m}{V}$: $d = \frac{12}{6}$

➔ <u>Answer:</u> **2 g/cm³**

Density – how squashed together the particles of a substance are

Mass – the amount of **matter** in a substance; measured in **grams**

Volume – the amount of **space** a substance takes up; measured in **milliliters (mL)** or **cubic centimeters (cm³)**

♦ <u>Example 2:</u> What is the *volume* of a brick with density of 8 g/cm³ and mass of 24 grams?

➔ $d = \frac{m}{V}$: $8 = \frac{24}{V}$

➔ Answer: **3 cm³**

---

1. *A bubble of air at the bottom of a lake rises to the surface of the lake. Data for the air inside the bubble at the bottom of the lake and at the surface of the lake are listed in the table to the right.*

   Determine the mass of the air in the bubble at the surface of the lake.

   Data for the Air Inside the Bubble

Location in Lake	Temperature (K)	Pressure (kPa)	Volume (mL)	Density (g/mL)
surface	293	104.0	2.5	0.0012
bottom	282	618.3	?	————

Mole Calculations	number of moles = $\dfrac{\text{given mass}}{\text{gram-formula mass}}$

The *Mole Calculations* equation allows you to figure out how many **moles (mol)** make up a specific element or compound. Sometimes, you are given the number of moles and must find either the mass or gram-formula mass.

➔ *Mole* → equal to 6.02×10^{23} particles (a **very** large number of particles!)

➔ *Given mass* → the mass of the given compound in grams

➔ *Gram-formula mass* → the total mass of the element or compound, expressed in g/mol (grams per mole). This can be found by finding the sum of the masses of all the atoms in the formula (found by rounding the atomic mass of each element to the nearest whole number), then expressing your answer in grams. Often, the gram-formula mass is also given to you.

♦ Example 1: What is the number of moles of HCl in a 108-gram sample of the compound?

➔ Formula: $number\ of\ moles = \dfrac{given\ mass}{gram-formula\ mass}$

➔ Mass is given to you: $number\ of\ moles = \dfrac{108}{g-f\ mass}$

➔ Gram-formula mass is not given. To figure it out, look up the atomic masses of H and Cl (the components of the compound HCl) on the **PT** and round them to the nearest whole numbers. Then add them. 1+35=**36**. This is your gram-formula mass. Substitute this value into your equation: $number\ of\ moles = \dfrac{108}{36}$

➔ Divide 108 by 36 to get the number of moles

➔ Answer: **3 mol**

♦ Example 2: Ascorbic acid has a molecular formula of $C_6H_8O_6$ and a gram-formula mass of 176 grams per mole. Determine the number of moles of vitamin C in an orange that contains 0.071 gram of vitamin C.

➔ Formula: $number\ of\ moles = \dfrac{given\ mass}{gram-formula\ mass}$

➔ Given mass and gram-formula mass are given to you; plug them into the correct places: $number\ of\ moles = \dfrac{0.071}{176}$

➔ Divide 0.071 by 176 to get the number of moles

➔ Answer: approximately **0.0004 mol**

♦ **Example 3:** Determine the mass of 5.20 moles of C_6H_{12} (gram-formula mass = 84.2 grams/mole).

➔ Formula: $number\ of\ moles = \dfrac{given\ mass}{gram-formula\ mass}$

➔ Number of moles and gram-formula mass are given to you; plug them into the correct places: $5.20 = \dfrac{given\ mass}{84.2}$

➔ Multiply 5.20 and 84.2 to get the given mass

➔ Answer: **437.84 g**

---

2. *During a laboratory activity, appropriate safety equipment was used, and safety procedures were followed. A laboratory technician heated a sample of solid $KClO_3$ in a crucible to determine the percent composition by mass of oxygen in the compound. The unbalanced equation and the data for the decomposition of solid $KClO_3$ are shown below.*

$$KClO_3(s) \rightarrow KCl(s) + O_2(g)$$

Lab Data and Calculated Results

Object or Material	Mass (g)
empty crucible and cover	22.14
empty crucible, cover, and $KClO_3$	24.21
$KClO_3$	2.07
crucible, cover, and KCl after heating	23.41
KCl	?
O_2	0.80

Based on the lab data, show a numerical setup (that means just set up your equation – don't actually give your answer) to determine the number of moles of O_2 produced. Use 32 g/mol as the gram-formula mass of O_2.

3. What is the number of moles of KF in a 29-gram sample of the compound?
   (1) 1.0 mol   (3) 0.50 mol
   (2) 2.0 mol   (4) 5.0 mol

4. What is the number of moles of CO_2 in a 220.-gram sample of CO_2 (gram-formula mass = 44 g/mol)?
   (1) 0.20 mol   (3) 15 mol
   (2) 5.0 mol   (4) 44 mol

5. *The diagram below represents a cylinder with a moveable piston containing 16.0 g of $O_2(g)$. At 298 K and 0.500 atm, the $O_2(g)$ has a volume of 24.5 liters.*

Determine the number of moles of $O_2(g)$ in the cylinder. The gram-formula mass of $O_2(g)$ is 32.0 g/mol.
_____ **moles**

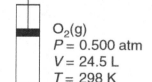

$O_2(g)$
P = 0.500 atm
V = 24.5 L
T = 298 K

Percent Error	$\% \ error = \dfrac{measured \ value - accepted \ value}{accepted \ value} \times 100$

Using the Formula:

♦ Be sure to follow **order of operations** when solving this equation. First subtract the accepted value from the measured value (because they are "grouped" together), then divide your answer by the accepted value, then multiply your result by 100.

♦ Sometimes, you need to look up the accepted value on **Table S** instead of having it provided for you.

♦ Express your answer as a **percentage**.

♦ **Note:** your answer will never be negative. If you get a negative result, *express it without the negative sign.*

> The ***Percent Error*** equation is used to determine how "off" a calculation/measurement is, based on a given **accepted** (actual) **value**. The higher the percent of error, the less accurate the calculation was.

♦ **Example 1:** A thermometer read 88.1°C. The actual temperature is 88.9°C. Determine the percent of error.

   → Formula: $\% \ error = \dfrac{measured \ value - accepted \ value}{accepted \ value} \times 100$

   → *Measured value* is 88.1. Accepted value is 88.9. Substitute these values into the equation, then calculate: $\% \ error = \dfrac{88.1 - 88.9}{88.9} \times 100$

     ⇨ Subtract: 88.1 – 88.9 = -0.08

     ⇨ Divide: -0.08/88.9 ≈ -0.009

     ⇨ Multiply by 100: -0.009 X 100 = -0.09

   → Answer: approximately **0.09%** (never express answer as negative number)

♦ **Example 2:** A student measures the mass and volume of a piece of aluminum to be 25.6 g and 9.1 cm³. Then, with these values, he calculated the density of aluminum. Based on Table S, what is the percent error of the student's calculated density of aluminum?

   → First find the student's calculated density (*measured value*) for aluminum:

     ⇨ Formula: $d = \dfrac{m}{v} : d = \dfrac{25.6}{9.1} : d \approx 2.8 \ g/cm^3$

➔ Then look up aluminum's density on Table S *(accepted value)*, under the density column on the far right. (Aluminum's atomic number is 13.)

⇨ The accepted value for the density of aluminum is 2.7 g/cm³

➔ Finally, substitute your values into the percent error equation and solve:

⇨ $\% \ error = \dfrac{2.8-2.7}{2.7} \times 100$

⇨ Subtract: 2.8 − 2.7 = 0.1

⇨ Divide: 0.1/2.7 = $0.\overline{037}$

⇨ Multiply by 100: $0.\overline{037}$ X 100 ≈ 3.7

➔ <u>Answer:</u> approximately **3.7%**

----

6. A student measures the mass and volume of a sample of aluminum at room temperature and calculates the density of Al to be 2.85 grams per cubic centimeter. Based on Table S, what is the percent error for the student's calculated density of Al?

   (1) 2.7%   (3) 5.6%
   (2) 5.3%   (4) 95%

7. *In a laboratory investigation, a student is given a sample that is a mixture of 3.0 grams of NaCl(s) and 4.0 grams of sand, which is mostly SiO₂(s)… In the first step, the student places the sample in a 250-mL flask. Then, 50. grams of distilled water are added to the flask… The student reports that 3.4 grams of NaCl(s) were recovered from the mixture.*

   Show a numerical setup for calculating the student's percent error.

8. In a laboratory activity, the density of a sample of vanadium is determined to be 6.9 g/cm³ at room temperature. What is the percent error for the determined value?

   (1) 0.15%   (2) 0.87% (3) 13%   (4) 15%

9. *In the late 1800s, Dmitri Mendeleev developed a periodic table of the elements known at that time. Based on the pattern in his periodic table, he was able to predict properties of some elements that had not yet been discovered. Information about one of these elements is shown in the table below.*

Some Element Properties Predicted by Mendeleev

Predicted Elements	Property	Predicted Value	Actual Value
eka-silicon (Es)	density at STP	5.5 g/cm³	5.3234 g/cm³
	melting point	high	938°C
	oxide formula	EsO₂	
	approximate molar mass	72 g/mol	

Show a numerical setup for calculating the percent error of Mendeleev's predicted density of Es.

Percent Composition	$\% \text{ composition by mass} = \dfrac{\text{mass of part}}{\text{mass of whole}} \times 100$

The ***percent composition*** equation expresses the fraction (the **"part"**) of given substance (element) within a specific compound or mixture (the **"whole"**), such as the percentage of oxygen (O) in water (H_2O).

"Percent composition by mass" means that the calculation is based on the *masses* of the parts and the wholes, not on the total number of atoms. Since oxygen has a much larger mass than hydrogen does (18 vs. 1), this means that oxygen's percent composition by mass in water is approximately 88%, not the 33% you would get by calculating the one oxygen atom vs. the three atoms that make up the entire water molecule.

Using the Formula:

- ***Mass of part*** → often given to you. Sometimes you need to look it (the element) up on the **PT**. (Round the **atomic mass** in the upper left corner to the nearest whole number.)

- ***Mass of whole*** → When the *whole* is a compound, its mass is usually provided for you in the gram-formula mass form (g/mol). (See **example 1** below.) When the *whole* is a mixture, you are usually provided with the mass of the part and the mass of the other part of the mixture, and you must add the two to get the entire mass. (See example 2 below.)

- <u>Example 1:</u> What is the percent composition by mass of hydrogen in NH_4HCO_3 (gram-formula mass = 79 grams/mole)?

  → Formula: $\% \text{ composition by mass} = \dfrac{\text{mass of part}}{\text{mass of whole}} \times 100$

    ⇒ Calculate *mass of part* (hydrogen) by looking up hydrogen's mass on the PT, then multiplying that number by the number of hydrogen atoms there are in the given compound. 1X5=5. *Mass of part* is **5 g**.

    ⇒ *Mass of whole* is **79 g** (given).

    ⇒ Calculate: $\% \text{ composition by mass} = \dfrac{5}{79} \times 100$

  → <u>Answer:</u> approximately **6.3%**

- <u>Example 2:</u> A sample of NaCl weighing 15 g was dissolved into 25 g of water, creating a saltwater solution. Calculate the percent composition by mass of the NaCl in the solution.

  → Formula: $\% \text{ composition by mass} = \dfrac{\text{mass of part}}{\text{mass of whole}} \times 100$

⇨ *Mass of part* (NaCl) is clearly **15 g**, as stated in the problem.

⇨ *Mass of whole* (saltwater solution) → the whole solution consists of NaCl weighing 15 g *plus* the 25 grams of water into which the NaCl is dissolved. Therefore, the *mass of whole* is 15 + 25, or **40 g**.

⇨ Calculate: $\% \; composition \; by \; mass = \frac{15}{40} \times 100$

→ Answer: **37.5%**

----

10. *In a lab activity, each of four different masses of $KNO_3(s)$ is placed in a separate test tube that contains 10.0 grams of H_2O at 25°C... The mixture in each test tube is then stirred while it is heated in a hot water bath until all the $KNO_3(s)$ is dissolved... The procedure is repeated until the recrystallization temperatures for each mixture are consistent, as shown in the table below.*

Determine the percent by mass concentration of KNO_3 in mixture 2 after heating.

Data Table for the Laboratory Activity

Mixture	Mass of KNO₃ (g)	Mass of H₂O (g)	Temperature of Recrystallization (°C)
1	4.0	10.0	24
2	5.0	10.0	32
3	7.5	10.0	45
4	10.0	10.0	58

11. A solution contains 25 grams of KNO_3 dissolved in 200. grams of H_2O. Which numerical setup can be used to calculate the percent by mass of KNO_3 in this solution?

(1) $\frac{25\,g}{175\,g} \times 100$

(2) $\frac{25\,g}{200.\,g} \times 100$

(3) $\frac{25\,g}{225\,g} \times 100$

(4) $\frac{200.\,g}{225\,g} \times 100$

12. What is the percent composition by mass of nitrogen in the compound N_2H_4 (gram-formula mass = 32 g/mol)?

(1) 13%   (3) 88%
(2) 44%   (4) 93%

13. Show a numerical setup for calculating the percent composition by mass of oxygen in Al_2O_3 (gram-formula mass = 102 g/mol).

14. *Some compounds of silver are listed with their chemical formulas in the table below.*

Silver Compounds

Name	Chemical Formula
silver carbonate	Ag_2CO_3
silver chlorate	$AgClO_3$
silver chloride	$AgCl$
silver sulfate	Ag_2SO_4

Show a numerical setup for calculating the percent composition by mass of silver in silver carbonate (gram-formula mass = 276 g/mol).

15. Which compound has the smallest percent composition by mass of chlorine?

(1) HCl   (3) LiCl
(2) KCl   (4) NaCl

Concentration	parts per million = $\dfrac{\text{mass of solute}}{\text{mass of solution}} \times 1\,000\,000$
	molarity = $\dfrac{\text{moles of solute}}{\text{liter of solution}}$

Concentration → a measure of how *concentrated* a solution is – how much **solute** (thing being dissolved) there is per unit of **solvent** (the medium [usually liquid] in which the solute is being dissolved).

There are **two ways to express concentration**:

➔ *Parts per million (ppm)* → tells you how many parts of solute there would be per million parts of solution.

➔ *Molarity (M)* → tells you how many moles of solute there are per liter of solution

Using the Formulas:

♦ These equations are easy to use – just be sure that when asked to determine the concentration of a solution, you use the *correct equation*:

➔ Often, the question will state directly: "What is the *molarity*..." or "...expressed in *parts per million*." Then simply use the equation mentioned by the question. (See **examples 1 and 2**)

➔ If not...

⇨ When units of mass are given in **moles** and **liters**, use the *molarity* equation.

⇨ Otherwise, use the *parts per million* equation.

✓ When using this equation, remember to *multiply your quotient by 1000000*.

♦ Sometimes you must solve for a different part of the equation. (See **example 3**.)

Example 1: A 2.0-liter aqueous solution contains a total of 3.0 moles of dissolved NH_4Cl at 25°C and standard pressure. Determine the molarity of the solution.

➔ Equation:
$$molarity = \frac{moles\ of\ solute}{liter\ of\ solution}$$

⇨ Moles of solute is **3.0 moles**; Liter of solution is **2.0**.

⇨ Calculate:
$$molarity = \frac{3}{2}$$

➔ Answer: 1.5 M (This means that there is 1.5 mol of NH_4Cl dissolved in every liter of solution.)

♦ **Example 2:** An aqueous solution has 0.0070 gram of oxygen dissolved in 1000. grams of water. What is the dissolved oxygen concentration of this solution in parts per million?

➔ Equation: $parts\ per\ million = \frac{mass\ of\ solute}{mass\ of\ solution} X\ 1{,}000{,}000$

⇨ Mass of solute is **0.0070 g**

⇨ Add solute and water to find mass of solution: 0.007 + 1000 = **1000.007**

⇨ Calculate: $parts\ per\ million = \frac{0.0070}{1000.007} X 1{,}000{,}000$

➔ Answer: approximately **7 ppm** (This means that for every million parts of water, there are 7 parts of dissolved oxygen.)

♦ **Example 3:** An aqueous solution contains 300. parts per million of KOH. Determine the number of grams of KOH present in 1000. grams of this solution.

➔ Equation: $parts\ per\ million = \frac{mass\ of\ solute}{mass\ of\ solution} X\ 1{,}000{,}000$

⇨ Parts per million is **300**

⇨ Mass of solution is **1000**

⇨ Calculate: $300 = \frac{mass\ of\ solute}{1000} X 1{,}000{,}000$

➔ Answer: **0.3 g**

---

16. What is the molarity of 0.50 liter of an aqueous solution that contains 0.20 mole of NaOH (gram-formula mass = 40. g/mol)?
    (1) 0.1 M (2) 0.2 M (3) 2.5 M (4) 0.4 M

17. What is the molarity of a solution that contains 0.500 mole of KNO_3 dissolved in 0.500-liter of solution?
    (1) 1 M   (2) 2 M   (3) 0.5 M   (4) 4 M

18. What is the concentration of AgCl in an aqueous solution that contains 1.2×10^{-3} gram of AgCl in 800. grams of the solution?
    (1) 1.2 ppm   (3) 7.2 ppm
    (2) 1.5 ppm   (4) 9.6 ppm

19. Which expression could represent the concentration of a solution?
    (1) 3.5 g   (3) 3.5 mL
    (2) 3.5 M   (4) 3.5 mol

20. A solution is prepared using 0.125 g of glucose, $C_6H_{12}O_6$, in enough water to make 250. g of total solution. The concentration of this solution, expressed in parts per million, is
    (1) 5.0×10^1 ppm   (3) 5.0×10^3 ppm
    (2) 5.0×10^2 ppm   (4) 5.0×10^4 ppm

21. What is the concentration of an aqueous solution that contains 1.5 moles of NaCl in 500. milliliters of this solution?
    (1) 0.30 M   (3) 3.0 M
    (2) 0.75 M   (4) 7.5 M

Combined Gas Law	$\dfrac{P_1 V_1}{T_1} = \dfrac{P_2 V_2}{T_2}$	P = pressure V = volume T = temperature

Combined Gas Law → demonstrates the relationships between **pressure**, **volume** and **temperature**. The equation shows what happens to one factor when either one or two of the other ones are changed.

Using the Formula:

♦ Although this equation is not difficult, since it includes so many variables, *it is easy to accidently mix them up* and end up with the wrong answer. Therefore, follow these steps to avoid confusion:

   1. As you read through the problem, **identify the 6 variables** and list them downwards in the same order as they are listed in the equation (**P_1, V_1, T_1, P_2, V_2, T_2**) along with their units. Place a question mark next to the unknown variable. (See **example 1** in the sidebar above.)

Example 1:

A rigid cylinder with a movable piston contains a 2.0-liter sample of neon gas at STP. What is the volume of this sample when its temperature is increased to 311 K while its pressure is decreased to 90. kilopascals?

1. P_1 = 101.3 kPa (STP – Table A)

   V_1 = 2.0 L

   T_1 = 273 K (STP – Table A)

   P_2 = 90 kPa

   V_2 = ?

   T_2 = 311 K

2. $\dfrac{P_1 V_1}{T_1} = \dfrac{P_2 V_2}{T_2}$

   $\dfrac{(101.3\ kPa)(2.0\ L)}{273\ K} = \dfrac{(90\ kPa)(V_2)}{311\ K}$

3. $V_2 \approx 2.6\ L$

It is not possible to use degrees Celsius when using STP, since standard temperature in Celsius (0) will cause all fractions to become *undefined*.

⇨**Pressure** is given in *kilopascals (kPa)* or *atmospheres (atm)*, **volume** is given in *milliliters/liters (mL/L)*, and **temperature** is usually given in *Kelvin (K)* but sometimes can be in *degrees Celsius (°C)* as well.

⇨If you are told that one or more variables are at **"STP"** (Standard Temperature and Pressure), use **Table A – STP** for these values. Note that Table A gives temperature and pressure in two different units:

   ✓ If the given pressure is in *kilopascals*, substitute **101.3 kPa** for the "STP pressure." If the given pressure is in *atmospheres*, substitute **1 atm** for the "STP pressure."

   ✓For temperature, *always use Kelvin*. If the given temperature is in °Celsius, *convert it to Kelvin* using the temperature conversion formula on **Table T**.

Table A
Standard Temperature and Pressure

Name	Value	Unit
Standard Pressure	101.3 kPa 1 atm	kilopascal atmosphere
Standard Temperature	273 K 0°C	kelvin degree Celsius

Temperature	$K = °C + 273$	K = kelvin °C = degree Celsius

2. **Substitute the values** you listed into the equation.

⇨ If one variable remains constant (does not change), simply leave it out. (See **example 2**.)

3. **Solve**.

♦ <u>Example 2:</u> A gas a STP has a volume of 4 L. If its volume was changed to 2 L and its temperature was changed to 298 K, what is its new volume?

1. <u>List variables in order:</u>

✓ P_1 = 101.3 kPa (STP)   ✓ P_2 = 101.3 kPa (didn't change)
✓ V_1 = 4 L   ✓ V_2 = ?
✓ T_1 = 273 K (STP)   ✓ T_2 = 298 K

2. <u>Substitute values</u> into the equation: $\frac{P_1 V_1}{T_1} = \frac{P_2 V_2}{T_2} \rightarrow \frac{(101.3\ kPa)(4\ L)}{273\ K} = \frac{(101.3\ kPa)V_2}{298\ K}$

Notice that pressure remained the same in both equations, so leave it out:
$\frac{(4\ L)}{273\ K} = \frac{V_2}{298\ K}$

3. <u>Solve:</u> $V_2 \approx \mathbf{4.4\ L}$

♦ <u>Example 3:</u> A 220.0-mL sample of helium gas is in a cylinder with a movable piston at 105 kPa and 275 K. The piston is pushed in until the sample has a volume of 95.0 mL. The new temperature of the gas is 310. K. What is the new pressure of the sample?

1. <u>List variables in order:</u>

✓ P_1 = 105 kPa   ✓ P_2 = ?
✓ V_1 = 220 mL   ✓ V_2 = 95 mL
✓ T_1 = 275 K   ✓ T_2 = 310 K

2. <u>Substitute values</u> into the equation: $\frac{P_1 V_1}{T_1} = \frac{P_2 V_2}{T_2} \rightarrow \frac{(105\ kPa)(220\ mL)}{275\ K} = \frac{P_2(95\ mL)}{310\ K}$

3. <u>Solve:</u> $P_2 \approx \mathbf{274\ kPa}$

22. *A 200.-milliliter sample of $CO_2(g)$ is placed in a sealed, rigid cylinder with a movable piston at 296 K and 101.3 kPa.*

    Determine the volume of the sample of $CO_2(g)$ if the temperature and pressure are changed to 336 K and 152.0 kPa.

23. A sample of a gas in a rigid cylinder with a movable piston has a volume of 11.2 liters at STP. What is the volume of this gas at 202.6 kPa and 300. K?

    (1) 5.10 L   (3) 22.4 L
    (2) 6.15 L   (4) 24.6

24. *The diagram below represents a cylinder with a moveable piston containing 16.0 g of $O_2(g)$. At 298 K and 0.500 atm, the $O_2(g)$ has a volume of 24.5 liters.*

    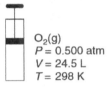

    $O_2(g)$
    $P = 0.500$ atm
    $V = 24.5$ L
    $T = 298$ K

    Show a numerical setup for calculating the volume of $O_2(g)$ in the cylinder at 265 K and 1.00 atm.

25. At standard temperature, 400 mL of a gas has pressure of 101.3 kPa. If the pressure is changed to 50.65 kPa, what will the temperature be if its new volume is 551 mL?

26. At 25°C, gas in a rigid cylinder with a movable piston has a volume of 145 mL and a pressure of 125 kPa. Then the gas is compressed to a volume of 80. mL. What is the new pressure of the gas if the temperature is held at 25°C?

    (1) 69 kPa   (3) 160 kPa
    (2) 93 kPa   (4) 227 kPa

27. A rigid cylinder with a movable piston contains a sample of hydrogen gas. At 330. K, this sample has a pressure of 150. kPa and a volume of 3.50 L. What is the volume of this sample at STP?

    (1) 0.233 L   (3) 4.29
    (2) 1.96 L   (4) 6.26 L

Titration	$M_A V_A = M_B V_B$	M_A = molarity of H⁺ $\quad$ M_B = molarity of OH⁻
		V_A = volume of acid $\quad\quad$ V_B = volume of base

Titration → a laboratory process in which the volume of a solution of known concentration (**molarity**) is used to determine the concentration of another solution.

➜ *Neutralization* → when there are equal amounts of H+ and OH- ions in a solution.

Using the Formula:

♦ Although this equation also is not difficult, *it is easy to accidently mix up the variables* and end up with the wrong answer. Therefore, follow these steps to avoid confusion:

    1. As you read through the problem, **identify the 4 variables** and list them downwards in the same order as they are listed in the equation (M_A, V_A, M_B, V_B) along with their units. Place a question mark next to the unknown variable. (See **example 1** in the sidebar above.)

      ⇨ **Molarity** is expressed in *M*.

        ✓ M_A → molarity of H⁺ – the acid. (Acids' formulas generally begin with H – see **Table K – Common Acids**.)

        ✓ M_B → molarity of OH⁻ – the base. (**Bases'** formulas generally end in **OH**. See **Table L – Common Bases**.) **Molarity** is given in *M*.

      ⇨ **Volume** is expressed in *milliliters (mL)*.

    2. Substitute the values you listed into the equation.

    3. Solve.

♦ <u>Example 2:</u> A student completes a titration by adding 12.0 milliliters of NaOH(aq) of unknown concentration to 16.0 milliliters of 0.15 M HCl(aq). What is the molar concentration of the NaOH(aq)?

Example 1:

In a titration, 20.0 milliliters of a 0.150 M NaOH(aq) solution exactly neutralizes 24.0 milliliters of an HCl(aq) solution. What is the concentration of the HCl(aq) solution?

1. **Identify variables:**
   - ✓ M_A = ? M
   - ✓ V_A = 24 mL (HCl is the acid – begins with H)
   - ✓ M_B = 0.150 M
   - ✓ V_B = 20.0 mL (NaOH is the base – ends with OH)

2. **Substitute** into equation:

$$M_A(24\ mL) = (0.150\ M)(20.0\ mL)$$

3. **Solve**:

$$M_A = 0.125\ M$$

1. List variables in order:
   - ✓ $M_A = 0.15$ M
   - ✓ $V_A = 16$ mL
   - ✓ $M_B = ?$ M
   - ✓ $V_B = 12$ mL

2. Substitute values into the equation:
   $$M_A V_A = M_B V_B \rightarrow (0.15\ M)(16\ mL) = M_B(12\ mL)$$

3. Solve: $M_B = 0.2\ M$

----

28. Which laboratory process is used to determine the concentration of one solution by using a volume of another solution of known concentration?

    (1) crystallization   (3) filtration
    (2) distillation   (4) titration

29. In a titration, 5.0 mL of a 2.0 M NaOH(aq) solution exactly neutralizes 10.0 mL of an HCl(aq) solution. What is the concentration of the HCl(aq) solution?

    (1) 1.0 M (2) 2.0 M (3) 10. M (4) 20. M

30. *In a laboratory investigation, an HCl(aq) solution with a pH value of 2 is used to determine the molarity of a KOH(aq) solution. A 7.5-milliliter sample of the KOH(aq) is exactly neutralized by 15.0 milliliters of the 0.010 M HCl(aq). Show a numerical setup for calculating the molarity of the KOH solution.*

31. *In a laboratory activity, a student titrates a 20.0-milliliter sample of HCl(aq) using 0.025 M NaOH(aq). In one of the titration trials, 17.6 milliliters of the base solution exactly neutralizes the acid sample.*
    Show a numerical setup for calculating the concentration of the hydrochloric acid using the titration data.

32. *Base your answers to this question on the table below.*

    Data for HCl(aq) Solutions

Solution	Concentration of HCl(aq) (M)	pH Value
W	1.0	0
X	0.10	1
Y	0.010	2
Z	0.0010	3

    Determine the volume of 0.25 M NaOH(aq) that would exactly neutralize 75.0 milliliters of solution X.

| Heat | $q = mC\Delta T$
 $q = mH_f$
 $q = mH_v$ | q = heat
 m = mass
 C = specific heat capacity
 ΔT = change in temperature | H_f = heat of fusion
 H_v = heat of vaporization |

Heat equations – help you figure out how much heat/energy is involved when there is a phase or temperature change.

There are **three heat equations**:

➔ $q = mC\Delta T$ – used for **temperature** changes – tells you, based on a substance's *specific heat capacity* (see Table B) how much heat is absorbed or released *when its temperature changes*

⇨ **C/specific heat capacity** → the amount of energy needed to raise 1 gram of a substance 1 Kelvin.

➔ $q = mH_f$ and $q = mH_V$ – used for **phase** changes:

⇨ $q = mH_f$ → melting/freezing ("fusion" = melting process) – tells you how much heat is required to *melt* a substance or how much heat will be released when the substance *freezes*.

⇨ $q = mH_V$ → evaporating/condensing ("vaporization" = evaporation) – tells you how much heat is required to *evaporate* a substance or how much heat will be released when the substance *condenses*.

Using the Formula:

1. Determine which formula of the three is the appropriate one <u>to use</u>:

➔ If the question mentions a temperature change, use the first equation.

➔ For a phase change – use either the second or third equation:

⇨ Melting or freezing: q = mH$_f$

⇨ Evaporating or condensing: q = mH$_v$

2. Identify & substitute the given values into the equation:

➔ Use **Table B – Physical Constants for Water** to look up the *Specific Heat Capacity* and *Heats of Fusion/Vaporization* of water. (Regents questions only refer to water when using these equations.)

Table B
 Physical Constants for Water

Heat of Fusion	334 J/g
Heat of Vaporization	2260 J/g
Specific Heat Capacity of $H_2O(\ell)$	4.18 J/g•K

3. Solve.

♦ <u>Example 1:</u> How much heat is absorbed when 30 g of water are heated 10 °C?

   1. <u>Determine the formula:</u>
       ✓ Since the question mentions a temperature change (*"are heated 10 °C"*), we know to use the first heat equation: $q = mC\Delta T$
   2. <u>Identify and substitute values into the equation:</u>
       ✓ q = ?
       ✓ m = 30 g
       ✓ C = 4.18 J (Table B)
       ✓ ΔT = 10 °C
       ✓ q = (30)(4.18)(10)
   3. <u>Solve:</u> q = **1254 J**

♦ <u>Example 2:</u> How much heat is released when 10 g of H_2O freezes?

   1. <u>Formula:</u> $q = mH_f$ (water is *freezing*)
   2. <u>Identify and substitute</u>
       ✓ m = 10 g
       ✓ H_f = 334 J (Table B)
       ✓ q = (10)(334)
   3. <u>Solve:</u> q = 3,340 J

♦ <u>Example 3:</u> 418 J are added to 10 g of water at 20° C. What is its new temperature?

   1. <u>Formula:</u> $q = mC\Delta T$ (*"What is its new temperature?"* indicates a temperature change.)
   2. <u>Identify and substitute:</u>
       ✓ q = 418
       ✓ m = 10 g
       ✓ C = 4.18 J (Table B)
       ✓ ΔT = ?
       ✓ 418 = (10)(4.18)ΔT
   3. <u>Solve:</u> ΔT = 10
       ✓ If ΔT (change in temp.) is 10, the new temperature must be **30 °C** (20 + 10)

♦ <u>Example 4:</u> How many joules are needed to vaporize 423 g of water at 100° C?

   1. <u>Formula:</u> $q = mH_v$ (water is *vaporizing)*
   2. <u>Identify and substitute:</u>
       ✓ m = 423
       ✓ H_v = 2260 J
       ✓ q = (423)(2260)
   3. <u>Solve:</u> q = **955,980 J**(75

33. What is the amount of heat absorbed when the temperature of 75 grams of water increases from 20.°C to 35°C?
    (1) 1100 J   (3) 6300 J
    (2) 4700 J   (4) 11 000 J

34. Which numerical setup can be used to calculate the heat energy required to completely melt 100. grams of $H_2O(s)$ at 0°C?
    (1) (100. g)(334 J/g)   (3) (100. g)(4.18 J/g•K)(0°C)
    (2) (100. g)(2260 J/g)   (4) (100. g)(4.18 J/g•K)(273 K)

35. What is the amount of heat, in joules, required to increase the temperature of a 49.5-gram sample of water from 22°C to 66°C?
    (1) 2.2×10^3 J   (3) 9.1×10^3 J
    (2) 4.6×10^3 J   (4) 1.4×10^4 J

36. As a 15.1-gram sample of a metal absorbs 48.75 J of heat, its temperature increases 25.0 K. What is the specific heat capacity of the metal?
    (1) 0.129 J/g•K   (3) 3.23 J/g•K
    (2) 1.95 J/g•K   (4) 7.74 J/g•K

37. Show a numerical setup for calculating the quantity of heat in joules required to completely vaporize 102.3 grams of $H_2O(\ell)$ at 100.°C and 1.0 atm.

Temperature	$K = °C + 273$	K = kelvin $°C$ = degree Celsius

Using the Formula:

♦ A common mistake involving this simple formula is mixing up the 2 variables and inserting values into the wrong place. Therefore, follow these steps to avoid confusion:

   1. Copy down the equation.
   2. Carefully insert the given temperature into the right place.
   3. Solve.

♦ Sometimes you may have to use **Table S – Properties of Selected Elements** to look up a specific element's boiling or melting point that you are being asked to convert into °C.

> This formula enables one to easily convert **kelvins** (K) to **degrees Celsius** (°C) and vice versa.

Example 1:

At 23°C, 85.0 grams of $NaNO_3(s)$ are dissolved in 100. grams of $H_2O(l)$.

Convert the temperature of the $NaNO_3(s)$ to kelvins.

   1. $K = °C + 273$
   2. $K = 23 + 273$
   3. $K = 303$

---

38. Convert the melting point of mercury to degrees Celsius.

39. A method used by ancient Egyptians to obtain copper metal from copper(I) sulfide ore was heating the ore in the presence of air. Later, copper was mixed with tin to produce a useful alloy called bronze. Convert the melting point of the metal obtained from copper(I) sulfide ore to degrees Celsius.

40. Cyclopropane, an isomer of propene, has a boiling point of −33 °C at standard pressure. Convert the boiling point of cyclopropane at standard pressure to kelvins.

41. *Base your answers to this question on the information below.*

Some Properties of Three Compounds at Standard Pressure

Compound	Boiling Point (°C)	Solubility in 100. Grams of H_2O at 20.°C (g)
ammonia	−33.2	56
methane	−161.5	0.002
hydrogen chloride	−84.9	72

Convert the boiling point of hydrogen chloride at standard pressure to kelvins.

ANSWERS

TO THE

ON THE

NEW YORK STATE

CHEMISTRY REFERENCE TABLES

Table B

1) 2 ($q = mC\Delta T$; $q = (75)(4.18)(15)$; $q \approx 4700$ J)

2) 3 ($q = mH_f$; $q = (200)(334)$; $q = 66800$)

3) 668 J ($q = mH_f$; $q = (2)(334)$; $q = 668$)

4) 113000 J ($q = mH_v$; $q = (50)(2260$; $q = 113000$)

5) $q = (102.3)(2260)$

Table E

1) 2 (Table E)

2) 3 (Table E)

3) 4 (Table E)

4) 1 (See Table E and rules for writing chemical formulas.)

5) 1 (See Table E and rules for writing chemical formulas.)

6) 1 (See Table E and rules for writing chemical formulas.)

7) 4 (The bond is between two ions. One is a polyatomic ion found on Table E. The other one is what is "leftover" in the compound.)

8) 3 (Compounds that contain polyatomic ions have both ionic and covalent bonding.)

9) 2 (Compounds that contain polyatomic ions have both ionic and covalent bonding.)

10) Carbonate / CO_3^{2-}

11) Ionic and covalent

12) Ionic and covalent

Table F

1) Ca^{2+} / Ca^{+2} *Note:* "Ca" / "Calcium" is not correct, since the question asked for the formula of the ion, not for the element symbol or name.

2) $AgClO_3$ / silver chlorate (the only soluble compound among the choices)

3) Ag^+ / Pb^+ / Hg_2^{2+}

4) 2 (AgCl is the only compound among the choices that is insoluble.)

5) 3 (CO_3^{2-} is insoluble unless combined with Group 1 ions or ammonium. Since Na^+ is a Group 1 ion, this makes the entire compound soluble.)

6) 1 (PO_4^{3-} is insoluble unless combined with Group 1 ions or ammonium.)

7) 4

Table G

1) 4-6 g (90-85=5 / 90-84=6 / 90-86=4)

2) According to Table G, the salt solution is unsaturated. / The 3.0 g of salt dissolved in 50. g of H_2O has a concentration less than the solubility of NaCl on Table G at 20.°C. / Table G indicates that the solubility of NaCl is greater than the amount in the sample. (At 20°C, 50 g of water can hold about 19 g of NaCl – and it only has 3 g. So, all the NaCl will dissolve.)

3) 15-18 g (Find the point that the 10°C line hits the SO_2 curve.)

4) The solubility at 1 atm increases as the temp. decreases. / As the temp. of the solution increases, the solubility of SO_2 decreases. / At lower temps, more SO_2 can dissolve. / indirect/inverse relationship

5) 3 (the only choice that falls below the curve at 10° C and 80 g of solute)

6) 12-16 g (The solution can hold approximately 83 grams – 13 more than is already dissolved.)

Table H

1) 2
2) 2
3) 1
4) 3
5) 2
6) 2 (*Find vapor pressure of propanone at 35°C, then move right until you hit the ethanol curve. Then move down to see temp.*)
7) 44-46°C
8) 48-52 kPa (*Go to 82.3°C and move up until you hit water curve. Then move left to see where hits vapor pressure axis.*)

Table I

1. 2 (*Bottom half of table since compound is dissolving - look for negative delta H values, which indicates exothermic reactions.*)
2. 1 (*Halve 66.4 since it's 1 mole, not 2.*)
3. 4 (*Double 84.0 since it's 2 moles, not 1.*)
4. 3 (*Answer can only be among choices 1 and 3, since the other 2 are endothermic - they absorb heat - don't release heat. Of the two, choice 3 releases more energy.*)
5. 3 (*Halve 3351.*)
6. 3 (*It's the only negative ΔH among the choices.*)
7. 4 (*Answer must have a positive delta H since question is about absorbing energy. Of choices 3 and 4, 4 has a greater delta H value.*)
8. 1 (*It is exothermic since the energy is on the right side of the arrow. Delta H is negative since it's exothermic. You can also find this equation on the table and see clearly that delta H is negative, which indicates an exothermic reaction.*)
9. 1 (*positive delta H*)

Table J

1) 4 (*above Ni*)
2) 3 (*above Sr*)
3) 1 (*Cl is above Br*)
4) 4 (*Zn is above H2*)
5) 1 (*between Zn and Mg*)
6) **Magnesium is more active than zinc. / The Zn is less active than Mg. / Mg is higher on Table J.**
7) **Li / Ba / Rb / Sr / K /Ca / Cs / Na**
8) **Zn is more active than Cu. / Zinc oxidizes more easily than copper. / Zn is a better reducing agent. / Cu is located below Zn on Table J.**
9) **Magnesium is more active than hydrogen. / H₂ is less active than Mg.**
10) **Cu / Ag / Au**
11) **Copper is less reactive than iron. / Cu below H₂ on Table J**
12) **Zinc is more active than hydrogen, but copper is less active than hydrogen. / On Table J, Zn is above H₂, and Cu is below H₂.**

Tables K & L

1) 3 (*Use Table L. 4 contains carbon so can't be a base although ends in OH. Choices 1, 2 and 3 all are found on Table K, Common Acids.*)
2) 4 (*Use Table K. 2 is like ethanoic acid's formula, but it is not identical.*)
3) 4 (*Acids and bases are electrolytes. Use Tables K and L to determine whether a possible choice is an acid or base.*)
4) 2 (*Use Table K.*)
5) 3 (*Use both tables K & L. Choice 3 is the only one that appears on either table. It's another form of carbonic acid, H_2CO_3(aq). Choice 4 cannot be a base because it contains carbon.*)

Table M

1) **4** (*Highest pH = most basic. The lower the molar concentration of H_3O^+ ions in a solution, the more basic it is. Solution D has the lowest concentration.*)

2) **4** (*KOH is classified as a base as per Table L. Bases have pHs greater than 7.*)

3) **1** (*Going from left to right on the pH scale, every value on the pH scale is decreased by a factor of ten from the one preceding it. Ex: A solution with a pH of 4 has a hydronium ion concentration ten times as strong as a solution with a pH of 5.*)

4) **1** (*Use Tables K and L to determine whether the compounds are acids or bases. Once determined that they're acids, use Table M to figure out whether acids will turn blue litmus red or red litmus blue. Litmus is red in solutions with pHs less than 4.5 → acids.*)

5) **2** (*See explanation for question 3 above. 2 values on the pH scale → a hundredfold increase/decrease.*)

6) **3** (*See questions 3 & 5 above.*)

7) **Blue** (*According to Table M, bromcresol green is blue in any solution with a pH > 5.4. Since KOH is a base, its pH is, at the very least, greater than 7 → definitely greater than 5.4.*)

8) **Yellow** (*As per Table M, since NH_3 is a base, it will turn methyl orange yellow.*)

9) **Methyl orange / bromthymol blue / thymol blue** (*Bromcresol green is yellow only in solutions with pHs less than 3.8.*)

10) **It has a pH of 3 / Its pH is less than 7**

11) **Bromthymol blue / bromcresol green / thymol blue**

12) **Methyl orange** (*Its color change range starts above 2 and ends below 5.*)

13) **The solution with a pH of 2 has a greater hydronium ion concentration.**

14) **Household ammonia** (*The higher the pH value, the lower the hydronium ion concentration.*)

15) **Litmus would be red in both tomato juice and vinegar, since it only turns blue in solutions with pHs greater than 8.3.**

16) **Lemon juice** (*Its pH value is 1 less than vinegar → ten times more acidic.*)

Tables N & O

1) **4** *(1 → ½ → ¼ → 1/8 → 1/16)*

2) **2** *(Table N)*

3) **3** *(4 half-lives passed; 48/4 = 12)*

4) **2** *(Table N)*

5) **1** *(3 half-lives passed; 3.9/3 = 1.3)*

6) **Gamma emissions have a stronger penetrating power. / Beta emissions have a weaker penetrating power.**

7) **15.8 years** *(3 half-lives X 5.271 y)*

8) **90 neutrons; 60 protons** *(lower number = nuclear charge/number of protons; higher number = mass number = sum of protons and neutrons)*

9) $^{81}_{33}As$ / **As-81** / **arsenic-81** / ^{81}As

10) **30.4 seconds** *(7.6 seconds X 4 half-lives)*

11) **U-238 and U-234 have the same number of protons, yet they have different numbers of neutrons.**

12) $^{0}_{-1}e$ / $^{0}_{-1}β$ / $β^-$ / **beta particle** *($^{234}_{90}Th →$ $^{234}_{91}Pa +$ _____)*

13) **The U-235 turns into two different elements during the reaction.** *(transmutation - when a radioisotope becomes a different element during its decay process)*

14) $^{97}_{41}Nb$ / **Nb-97** / **niobium-97** / ^{97}Nb

15) **Used in devices that eliminate static electricity in machinery / used in brushes to remove dust from camera lenses** *(This info is found in the introductory paragraph.)*

16) **3.5 milligrams** *(3 half-lives passed)*

17) $^{0}_{+1}e$ / $^{0}_{+1}β$ / **B+** / **positron** *(Tables N & O)*

18) **They each have the same number of protons as they have electrons.**

19) $^{0}_{-1}e$ / $^{0}_{-1}β$ / $β^-$ / **beta particle** *(Tables N & O)*

Table Q

1) **1** *(Ethene is an alkene, whose general formula matches choice 1.)*

2) **3** *(A hydrocarbon - so must be either choice 2 or 3. One triple bond - so choice 3.)*

3) **1** *(Butane is an alkane, which is saturated. Alkenes and alkynes are unsaturated.)*

4) **4** *(See GENERAL FORMULA column on Table Q.*

5) **2** *(The other three choices are alkanes - they have 2n+2 H for every C.)*

6) **3** *(Follows alkyne general formula of C_nH_{2n-2}.)*

7) **1** *(4 carbons [so prefix but-] and 10 hydrogens - matches alkane general formula of C_nH_{2n+2}.)*

8) **Carbon**

9) **Hydrocarbons contain only carbon and hydrogen, but compound B also contains oxygen. / Compound B contains carbon, hydrogen, and a different element. / This compound includes oxygen.**

Table R

1) **3** (Using Table R, you see that the molecule contains the amine functional group [N], which is 1st in the C chain. You also see that there are 5 carbons → pent-. [Table P])

2) **3** (See 1 above. There are 4 carbons here → but-.)

3) **4** (Not stated on the table, but you should be able to figure out from all the examples that all organic compounds contain carbon...)

4) **2**

5) **4**

6) **Acceptable answers include:**

Examples of 1-credit responses:

7) **Acceptable answers include:**

Examples of 1-credit responses

8) **C/Carbon**

9) **Ester(s)** (Has O=C-O functional group, ends in -anoate.)

10) **Alcohol** (Has OH functional group.)

11) **Alcohol** (OH functional group)

12) **A 1-credit response:**

13) **Halide / Halocarbon** (Cl functional group)

The Periodic Table (Part I)

1) **4** (Look at the last number of each element's electron configuration on the lower left of its box, which represents the element's valence electrons.)

2) **4** (Look up chlorine's electron configuration on the periodic table, which is its electron configuration in ground state, and compare it to the choices. Cl has an electron configuration of 2-8-7 in ground state. So, choice 2 is out. Now look for a choice that has the same total number of electrons as choice 2 but is arranged in a different setup → choice 4.)

3) **2** (because there are three shells, but the second shell isn't full yet)

4) **1** (Look up sodium's electron configuration on the PT – atomic #11.)

5) **1**

6) **1** (Write the elements' symbols and oxidation states. (II) means use +2 for iron's oxidation state: $Fe^{+2}O^{-2}$. Crisscross and omit charges: Fe_2O_2. Simplify: FeO.)

7) **3** (42 is potassium's mass number → sum of its protons and neutrons. To find the number of neutrons, subtract its number of protons from its mass number: 42 – 19 = 23.)

8) **Ne-20: 10, Ne-22: 12** (Neon's atomic number is 10. Subtract: 20 – 10 = 10; 22 – 10 = 12.)

9) **Two** (If atom D has 12 protons, then it also has 12 electrons. Its first shell must have 2, and its second shell must have 8. There are 2 electrons left for its 3rd and last shell – its valence electrons.)

10) **An electron in the first shell of an atom of isotope E has less energy than an electron in the second shell. / In an atom of E, an electron in the 2nd energy level has more energy than an electron in the 1st energy level. / Electrons in shell 2 have higher energies than shell 1 electrons. / lower in shell 1**

The Periodic Table (Parts II & III)

11) 4

12) 1

13) 2 (the only metal among the choices)

14) 2 (The number of valence electrons affects the chemical properties of an element. Choice 2 describes Ca's valence electrons.)

15) 3

16) 1 (Use Table S.)

17) 4 (Fluorine and chlorine are gases. You know that either by memorization or by using Tables A and S to figure it out. See Table S.)

18) 1 (Helium is a noble gas.)

19) 3 (As seen on Table S, fluorine, in Group 17, has the highest electronegativity.)

20) 4 (Oxygen is a nonmetal, and thus gains electrons to become stable. As seen on the PT, oxygen's normal electron configuration is (2-6). When it becomes an ion, it gains two electrons and has a configuration like neon's → (2-8).)

21) 2

22) 3 (See electron configuration of each group among the choices.)

23) 2

24) 1

25) 2

26) 2

27) Electronegativity generally decreases as the metals in Group 2 are considered in order of increasing atomic number. / Electronegativity decreases.

28) An atom of Ba has three more electron shells than an atom of Mg, so less energy is required to remove one of the outermost electrons from an atom of Ba. / Barium atoms have more inner shell electrons, resulting in a greater shielding effect. / Magnesium's valence electrons are closer to the nucleus. / Barium has a larger atomic radius.

29) Ionization energy increases. (Use Table S.)

30) Na, Mg, Al/aluminum, sodium, magnesium

31) Na/sodium (has the lowest first ionization energy)

32) As the atomic number of the elements in Period 3 increases, the atomic radius generally decreases. / The radius gets smaller. (Use Table S.)

33) In the ground state, the atomic radius of an iodine atom is smaller than the atomic radius of a rubidium atom. / The Rb atom is larger than the I atom. / The Rb atomic radius is 215 pm, but the I atomic radius is only 136 pm. (Use Table S.)

34) Krypton

Table S

1) **2** (Elements cannot be broken down chemically. The other three choices aren't elements – you won't find them on the PT or Table S.)

2) **1** (Ammonia is the only choice that isn't listed on Table S, since it's not an element.)

3) **1** (298 K and 1 atm is STP. Use density column and compare the choices.)

4) **2** (Use melting point and boiling point columns. 1000 K falls between aluminum's melting point of 933 K and boiling point of 2792 K, so aluminum would be liquid at this temp.)

5) **1** (Use the electronegativity column. Look up the electronegativities of each element that makes up the compounds in the choices: H, I, F, Cl, Br. Then find the difference of each pair. The least polar molecule will have the smallest difference.)

6) **4** (Use atomic radius column.)

7) **3**

8) **3**

9) **3** (Use the electronegativity column.)

10) **2** (Use the electronegativity column. See question 5.)

11) **4** (Use the melting point column.)

12) **2**

13) **Polar covalent / covalent / polar covalent bond** (Covalent since the difference between hydrogen and nitrogen's electronegativities is < 1.7.)

14) **Gas** (Standard temp. is 273 K – See Table A: Standard Temp. and Pressure. Since chlorine's boiling point is below this temp., at only 239 K, it is a gas.)

15) **Ge / Germanium** (Use the density column to find the element that has eka-silicon's density of 5.3234 g/cm3.

Notice that eka-silicon's given melting point is in degrees Celsius instead of in Kelvins, so in order to use the melting point column, you would first need to convert 938 °C into K by using the temp. conversion equation on Table T.)

Table T

1) **0.003 grams** ($d = \frac{m}{V}$: $0.0012 = \frac{m}{2.5}$: $m = 0.003$ g)

2) **Acceptable answers include:**

$$\frac{0.80\,g}{32\,g/mol}$$

$$\frac{0.80}{32}$$

$$.8g \times \frac{1\,mol}{32\,g}$$

$$\frac{1\,mol}{32\,g} = \frac{x\,mol}{0.80\,g}$$

(number of moles = $\frac{given\ mass}{gram-formula\ mass}$: number of moles = $\frac{0.80}{32}$)

3) **3** (number of moles = $\frac{given\ mass}{gram-formula\ mass}$: number of moles = $\frac{29}{gram-formula\ mass}$: to figure out gram formula mass, add masses of K [39] and F [19] → 58 g/mol: divide 29 by 58 to get 0.50 mol)

4) **2** (number of moles = $\frac{given\ mass}{gram-formula\ mass}$: number of moles = $\frac{220}{44}$)

5) **0.500 mol** (number of moles = $\frac{given\ mass}{gram-formula\ mass}$: number of moles = $\frac{16.0}{32.0}$)

6) **3** (% error = $\frac{2.85-2.7}{2.7} \times 100$)

7) **Acceptable answers include:**

$$\frac{3.4\ g - 3.0\ g}{3.0\ g} \times 100$$

$$\frac{(0.4)(100)}{3}$$

Note: Do *not* allow credit if the fraction is not multiplied by 100.

8) **4** (Look up vanadium's density on Table S – atomic number 23. Its density

is 6. Substitute this value as the "accepted value" part of the equation:
$\% \ error = \frac{6.9-6}{6} \times 100$)

9) Acceptable answers include:

$$\frac{5.5 \ \text{g/cm}^3 - 5.3234 \ \text{g/cm}^3}{5.3234 \ \text{g/cm}^3} \times 100$$

$$\frac{(5.5 - 5.3)(100)}{5.3}$$

$$\frac{0.2}{5.3} \times 100$$

10) **Allow 1 credit for 33% or any value from 33% to 33.3% inclusive.** (mass of part is 5.0. mass of whole is 15 [5.0 + 10.0]. When substituting these values into the formula, you get approximately 33%.)

11) **3** (% composition = $\frac{mass \ of \ part}{mass \ of \ whole} \times 10 \rightarrow 25$ g represents the mass of part and 225 g represents the mass of whole [25 g of KNO_3^+ 200 g of water])

12) **3** (Figure out mass of N_2 using the Periodic Table. [Round nitrogen's atomic mass – upper left corner – to the nearest whole number and multiply your answer by 2, since there are two nitrogen atoms. Then substitute this mass into the percent composition equation and solve: % composition = $\frac{28}{32} \times 100$)

13) Acceptable answers include:

$$\frac{3(16 \ \text{g/mol})}{102 \ \text{g/mol}} \times 100$$

$$\frac{(15.9994 \times 3)(100)}{102}$$

$$\frac{48}{102} \times 100$$

(Look up oxygen's mass on the PT. It is nearly 16. Multiply that by three since there are 3 oxygen atoms in the given formula. This is the mass of part. Mass of whole is 102 g, since it's the gram-formula mass of the entire compound.)

14) **Acceptable answers include:**

$$\frac{2(108 \ \text{g/mol})}{276 \ \text{g/mol}} \times 100$$

$$\frac{(216)(100)}{276}$$

$$\frac{2(107.868)}{275.7452} \times 100$$

(Look up silver's mass on the PT. It is nearly 108. Multiply that by two since there are 3 silver atoms in the given formula. This is the mass of part. Mass of whole is 276 g, since it's the gram-formula mass of the entire compound.)

15) **2** (Calculate the mass of whole of each of the choices by looking up each part of the compound's mass and then adding them to determine the entire compound's mass. For example, add 1 (mass of H) and 35 (mass of Cl) to get HCl's mass. Then calculate the percent composition of chlorine in the compound by using the formula.)

16) **4** (Use the molarity equation since the question asks for the molarity of the solution: moles of solute = 0.20; liters of solution = 0.50; substitute values into molarity equation → 0.4 M)

17) **1** (molarity equation: moles of solute = 0.500; liters of solution = 0.500 → 1.00 M)

18) **2** (parts per million equation: mass of solute = 0.0012 g [move decimal three times to the left]; mass of solution = 800 g; divide then multiply by 1,000,000 → 1.5 ppm)

19) **2** (Molarity, which measures concentration, is expressed as M.)

20) **2** (Use the parts per million equation since the question says, "expressed in parts per million:" mass of solute = 0.125 g; mass of solution = 250; divide then multiply by 1,000,000 → 500 ppm.

Answers

The choices are expressed in scientific notation... So, expand each choice [Take the ten's exponent and add that number of zeroes to the 5] and figure out which one is equivalent to your answer.)

21) **3** *(Use the molarity equation since the solute's mass is expressed in moles, and the solution's mass is expressed in (milli)liters. Now it gets tricky: You may have mistakenly divided 1.5 by 500. This is incorrect, however, since the formula asks specifically for the solution's volume in liters, and in this problem, it's expressed in milliliters. Therefore, you must convert 500 milliliters to its equivalent measure in liters. Use Table C – Selected prefixes to figure out how many milliliters are in one liter. It tells you that the prefix milli- represents a factor of 10-3, or 0.001. Move the decimal 3 times to the left and now you have 0.500 liters. Divide 1.5 by 0.500 → 3.0 M.)*

22) **151-151.4 mL** $\left(\frac{(101.3\ kPa)(200\ mL)}{296\ K} = \frac{(152\ kPa)V_2}{336\ K}\right)$

23) **2** *(Use Table A for STP values:* $\frac{(101.3\ kPa)(11.2\ L)}{273\ K} = \frac{(202.6\ kPa)V_2}{300\ K}$*)*

24) **Acceptable answers include:**

$$V = \frac{(24.5\ L)(265\ K)(0.500\ atm)}{(298\ K)(1.00\ atm)}$$

$$\frac{(0.500\ atm)(24.5\ L)}{298\ K} = \frac{(1.00\ atm)V}{265\ K}$$

$$\frac{(24.5)(265)(0.5)}{298}$$

25) **188** $\left[\frac{(101.3\ kPa)(400\ mL)}{273\ K} = \frac{(551\ mL)(50.65\ kPa)}{T_2}\right]$

26) **4** *[Leave out the temp. because it remains constant:* $(125\ kPa)(145\ mL) = P_2(80)$*]*

27) **3** *(Use Table A for STP values:* $\frac{(150\ kPa)(3.50\ L)}{330\ K} = \frac{(101.3\ kPa)V_2}{273\ K}$*)*

28) **4**

29) **1** $[M_A(10\ mL) = (2\ M)(5\ mL)]$

30) **Acceptable answers include:**

$$\frac{(0.010\ M)(15.0\ mL)}{7.5\ mL}$$

$$(0.010\ M)(15.0\ mL) = M_B\ (7.5\ mL)$$

$$\frac{(0.01)(15)}{7.5}$$

31) **Acceptable answers include:**

$$M_A(20.0\ mL) = (0.025\ M)(17.6\ mL)$$

$$\frac{(.025)(17.6)}{20}$$

32) **30 mL** $[(0.10\ M)(75\ mL) = (0.25\ M)V_B]$

33) **2** $[q = mC\Delta T \rightarrow q = (75\ g)(4.18\ J)(15\ °C)]$

34) **1** $[q = mH_f]$

35) **3** $[q = mC\Delta T \rightarrow q = (49.5\ g)(4.18\ J)(44\ °C) \rightarrow q \approx 9{,}100\ J$ *Choices are given in scientific notation, but you should be able to match your answer to the only answer choice that makes sense...]*

36) **1** $[q = mC\Delta T \rightarrow 48.75\ J = (15.1\ g)(C)(25\ K)]$

37) **q = (102.3 g)(2260 J/g) / 2260 X 102.3**

38) **-39** $[234 = °C + 273]$

39) **1085** $[1358 = °C + 273]$

40) **240** $[K = -33 + 273]$

41) **188.1** $[K = -84.9 + 273]$

MORE
PRACTICE

- See the charts on the next two pages for additional practice regents questions, organized by table and by regents.

- Not all questions in the chart are based entirely on the reference tables. Some questions also require some background knowledge not contained on the tables.

- Many questions may require the use of more than one table from the Chemistry Reference Tables. In that case, you'll find the question number listed twice, once under each table.

- By examining the table carefully, you'll notice that some tables appear on every regents multiple times (so they're worth reviewing!), while others have only appeared a few times in total on recent exams.

- To obtain the regents referenced on the chart, either use a recent Barron's review book or go to www·nysedregents·org/chemistry.

Table		Jan '15	Jun '15	Aug '15	Jan '16	Jun '16	Aug '16	Jan '17	Jun '17
A	Standard Temperature. and Pressure		46			11, 12		5, 52, 60	
B	Physical Constants for Water	71			39	58	41	40	76
C&D	Selected Prefixes Selected Units	18							16
E	Selected Polyatomic Ions			69	11	6		34	34
F	Solubility Guidelines for Aqueous Solutions		44	77	14	7		39	53
G	Solubility Curves at Standard Pressure		52		81	42	52		82
H	Vapor Pressure of Four Liquids			51	51				
I	Heats of Reaction at 101.3 kPa and 298 K	22			32				
J	Activity Series					80	66		
K, L, M	Common Acids; Common Bases; Common Acid-Base Indicators	41, 64	24, 81	61	27	49, 61	26, 47, 77	79	30, 84
N, O	Selected Radioisotopes; Symbols Used in Nuclear Chemistry	2, 29, 48, 83	1, 62, 64	1, 29, 64, 84	1, 30, 41	28, 29, 82	29	29, 83	4, 46, 64, 72
P, Q, R	Organic Prefixes; Homologous Series of Hydrocarbons; Organic Functional Groups	59, 76	7, 17, 18, 48, 69	21, 23, 45, 79	22, 47, 76, 77	22, 23, 45, 47, 77	43, 57, 81, 85	22, 45, 74, 76	25, 27, 44, 61, 66, 74
PT, S	The Periodic Table of the Elements Properties of Selected Elements	6, 11, 13, 16, 31, 32, 34, 44, 59, 63, 66-68, 85	3, 6, 8, 16, 20, 22, 23, 31, 33-36, 55, 66, 67	2, 5, 6, 10, 12, 15, 32-36, 38, 39-40, 55, 63	2, 5, 6, 8, 31, 33, 34, 40, 53, 60, 61, 68, 70, 85	3, 5, 9, 12, 31, 33-36, 49, 51, 67, 68, 72, 83, 84	2, 3, 6, 7, 9, 10, 12, 15, 31, 33, 36, 38, 60, 62, 63, 65	4-7, 10, 11, 15, 31, 37, 51, 52, 84	3, 6, 11-13, 31, 34 , 47, 51, 54, 57, 67, 74
T	Important Formulas and Equations	11, 43, 47, 54, 70, 71, 73, 80	12, 28, 39, 41, 46, 51, 56, 63, 77	42, 43, 48, 66	13, 38, 39, 52, 62, 65	11, 37, 46, 55, 58, 59, 64, 69	17, 40, 41, 50, 59, 71, 80	40, 41, 54-57, 60, 64	33, 50, 63, 70, 71, 76, 81

Table		Aug '17	Jan '18	Jun '18	Aug '18	Jan '19	Jun '19	Aug '19	Jan '20
A	Standard Temperature and Pressure	55				40	41		
B	Physical Constants for Water	40, 41	53		41	41		57	13
C & D	Selected Prefixes Selected Units								
E	Selected Polyatomic Ions		5, 67		34	34	66	34	36
F	Solubility Guidelines for Aqueous Solutions	11	38	56			71		
G	Solubility Curves at Standard Pressure	37			59, 60	67	56	59	72
H	Vapor Pressure of Four Liquids		42	13				58	80
I	Heats of Reaction at 101.3 kPa and 298 K	35	44	44	69		18	43	
J	Activity Series	44	80	49	47	25		47	46
K, L, M	Common Acids; Common Bases; Common Acid-Base Indicators	27	24, 54	84	81	26	27, 82	26-28	24, 71
N, O	Selected Radioisotopes; Symbols Used in Nuclear Chemistry	3, 84	64	28, 57-59	3, 28	55, 84	54, 63, 65	3, 84	20, 27, 48, 65
P, Q, R	Organic Prefixes; Homologous Series of Hydrocarbons; Organic Functional Groups	42, 60, 73	20, 42, 45, 83, 84	18, 21, 45, 53, 70, 76	21, 22, 35, 44, 75, 76, 77	23, 24, 43, 77-79	25, 45, 46, 51, 74, 76	22, 23, 45, 79, 81	18, 43, 63, 77, 82
PT, S	The Periodic Table of the Elements; Properties of Selected Elements	5-9, 13, 15, 31-34, 45, 48, 51, 54- 58, 61-64, 74, 83	3-5, 10, 14, 32, 34, 35-37, 39, 51, 52, 58, 67, 68	4, 6, 9-11, 14, 32, 34-36, 41, 51, 52, 58, 66-68	5, 6, 8, 9, 15, 25, 32-34, 39, 51, 54, 55-58, 61-63, 67, 82, 84	3, 5-8, 14, 34, 51, 53, 56, 58-63	5, 8, 13, 32-35, 38, 64, 66, 77	5-8, 11, 12, 14, 32, 36, 51-54, 68-71, 82, 85	4-6, 10, 11, 32, 33, 35, 36, 40, 51, 64, 67-69
T	Important Formulas and Equations	38-42, 45, 51, 64, 68, 70	25, 36, 39, 51, 53, 55, 62, 63, 65, 66, 69, 71, 72, 82	36, 39, 51, 55, 62, 63, 65, 69, 71, 72, 82	38-42, 51, 45, 68, 70	36-38, 40, 41, 57, 69, 81	33, 37, 41, 55, 59, 67, 72, 84	39, 57, 63, 67, 73-75	13, 35, 47, 57, 61, 76

Thanks for reading!

I'd love to hear how this book helped you understand any part of the Chemistry Reference Tables better than you did before.

Please email your comments or questions to bondingcrt@gmail.com.

I welcome your feedback!

Y. Finkel